DOG LOGIC
Companion
Obedience

The author and friends, Cerchie, Chattan and Smokey (*left to right*). All are titled CDX, Chattan has his first Schutzhund title and Chattan and Smokey are certified Police Service K-9s.

DOG LOGIC

Companion Obedience

Rapport-Based Training

JOEL M. McMAINS

HOWELL
BOOK HOUSE
New York

Macmillan General Reference
A Simon & Schuster Macmillan Company
1633 Broadway
New York, NY 10019-6785

Library of Congress Cataloging-in-Publication Data

McMains, Joel M.
Dog logic—companion obedience : rapport-based training / Joel M. McMains.
p. cm.
Includes index.
ISBN 0-87605-510-2
1. Dogs—Training. I. Title.
SF431.M467   1992   92-925
636.7′0887—dc20   CIP

10 9 8 7 6

Printed in the United States of America

We can only know
what is *out there*
from an animal's features

for we make even infants
turn and look back
at the way things are shaped

not toward the open
that lies so deep
in an animal's face.

Rainer Maria Rilke
Eighth Elegy, *Duino Elegies*

For my parents, who introduced me to *Canis familiaris*. And for Bud Swango—no one has had a truer friend.

Contents

Acknowledgments

―――――――――――――――――――――――

T HIS PROJECT never could have come to fruition without help from several individuals. For her beautiful photography and
knowledgeable suggestions, I thank Mary McMains. For their invaluable
insights, I thank friends and confidants Ron Flath, Jo Sykes, Roger David-
son, Jim Robinson, Sharon Michael, Linda Slack, Brenda Powell, Barb
Ketcham, Bill and Barb Ziegler and my special adviser, H.P.

I extend my deep appreciation to those authors and instructors who
have taught me and to my primary teachers: every dog I've ever known.
I feel special gratitude for a German Shepherd named Hawkeye, another
called Smokey, a Doberman Pinscher named Chattan, a small, furry
crossbreed named Charlie and, perhaps most, for a Standard Poodle called
Cinnabar, who taught me about dignity. They welcomed me and showed
me. I am beholden beyond words to them all.

Foreword

DOG BREEDERS sometimes suffer from a malady known as *kennel blindness*. The presence of the affliction may be suspected when an otherwise knowledgeable dog person can find no fault with any dog in his own kennel. Dog obedience instructors not infrequently come down with a related virus. The only way to train a dog is their way.

In my thirty-plus years as an obedience instructor, I have experimented with the ideas of many trainers. Some of their methods I have adopted; others I have rejected. Six years ago I ran into Joel McMains of Sheridan, Wyoming. Joel takes a view of dog obedience training unlike any other. He realizes that no one method is the best approach to every kind and condition of dog, and he speaks a new, delightful heresy. Excellence in the ring is not a goal, merely one of the fringe benefits to be gained from obedience training. Joel is not much interested in the handler who neither knows nor cares about the workings of his canine co-worker's mind.

Dog Logic is a book of methods, ideas and philosophy. No, Joel is not a wishy-washy, train-'em-with-love instructor. Love, yes, but discipline, consistency and a generous application of common sense. Joel does not correct for honest mistakes, nor does he expect a dog to know what it has not been taught.

Whatever the stage of your dog's training, you will find value in this volume. McMains's methods are psychologically sound. They produce happy, confident and accurate workers that excel as full-time companions as well as in the obedience ring.

Yup, I'm beginning to suffer from a mutant strain of kennel blindness. I can't find much fault with Joel McMains's approach to dog obedience training.

Jo Sykes
Livingston, Montana

Preface

THIS IS a book about dog obedience training. Like all such books, it is a work of opinion and conjecture: The only ones that can finally know are the dogs themselves.

The text proceeds on the premise that the reader may not know the collar end of a dog from the noncollar end. While that presumption may cause experienced trainers to foresee periods of nodding off, I hope they can approach the text with an open mind. It offers concepts and techniques that may not be encountered elsewhere.

Of course, similarities exist between certain of my methods and those of other trainers-authors. That's because several good obedience books are available. I don't claim to have discovered a *revolutionary path to the only true way!* The market offers an adequate supply of those, too.

Experienced hands, however, will note dissimilarities between my training approaches and those of other writers. My specific approach is neither a spoon-fed formula nor a rehash of contemporary wisdom. It neither insults reader intelligence nor exhorts established decrees at every juncture. The books debunk several popular misconceptions about canines and their training. They add to and subtract from the base of common knowledge, the purpose being to open doors.

Dog Logic gives readers the "whys" as well as the "hows" of training and methods; why a certain technique is effective while another falls flat. In many instances, the books explain what goes on inside a dog's head, so to speak. The hope is that you'll come away with not merely a teaching agenda but a deeper understanding of how dogs learn, how they assimilate information.

Unlike a good many within the genre, the texts are not formatted exclusively along American Kennel Club (AKC) obedience standards. As a professional trainer, I operate from a different perspective than that of a participant in AKC obedience trials. Not better: different. Training is my livelihood, not a hobby. My reputation rides on every dog I touch. I have to consistently produce reliable, happy workers or I'm not only out of the ribbons; I'm out of business. *Advanced Obedience—Easier Than You Think* outlines my approaches to various titles, but that material is offered peripherally, not as a focal point. Competition is best viewed as but one possible expression of a thoroughly schooled dog, not as an end in itself.

While the mechanics of training are well covered, my writing is just as concerned with the human-canine relationship as it is with the training process. It deals with perceptions and attitudes as well as with procedures and methods and examines traps to which the unwary can fall prey. I am also mindful that many owners have limited time to devote to training.

The books can serve the general obedience needs of training levels from family pet to competitor to working service dog. Their purposes are to teach about canine ways and to aid in producing trained animals that are within their handler's control, are dependable, and are happy.

Whether you're a beginner, a seasoned pro or are somewhere in between, take a moment to peruse the article ''A Tribute to the Dog'' presented on the following page. Its essence is bedrock to the relationship you and your companion must develop if the two of you are to discover and develop anything of a worthwhile and enduring nature.

A Tribute to the Dog

IN 1870, a young lawyer practicing law in a small Missouri town was representing a man who was suing another for damages amounting to $200 for wantonly killing his dog, Old Drum. He paid no attention to the testimony. When it came time for his summation, he addressed the court:

"Gentlemen of the jury: The best friend a man has in this world may turn against him and become his enemy. His son or his daughter that he has reared with loving care may prove ungrateful. Those who are nearest and dearest to us, those whom we trust with our happiness and our good name, may become traitors to their faith. The money that a man has he may lose. It flies away from him, perhaps when he needs it most. The people who are prone to fall on their knees to do us honor when success is with you may be the first ones to throw the stone of malice when failure settles its cloud upon our heads.

"The one absolutely unselfish friend that a man can have in this selfish world, the one that never deserts him, the one that never proves ungrateful or treacherous, is his dog. A man's dog stands by him in prosperity and in poverty, in health and in sickness. He will sleep on the cold ground, where the wintry winds blow and the snow drives fiercely, if only he may be near his master's side. He will kiss the hand that has no food to offer; he will lick the wounds and sores that come with the roughness of the world. He guards the sleep of his pauper master as if he were a prince. When all other friends desert, he alone remains. When riches take wings and reputation falls to pieces, he is as constant in his love as the sun in its journey through the heavens.

"If fortunes drive the master forth an outcast in the world, friendless and homeless, the faithful dog asks for no higher a privilege than that of accompanying him, to guard him against danger, to fight against his enemies. And when the last scene of all comes and death takes his master in its embrace and his body is laid away in the cold ground, no matter if all other friends pursue the way, there by the graveside will be found the noble dog, his head between his paws and his eyes sad, but open in alert watchfulness, faithful and true, even in death."

He won the case. The jury deliberated for two minutes, then awarded $500 in damages to the plaintiff.

George Graham Vest went on to serve for twenty-four years in the U.S. Senate as one of that body's leading orators and debaters.

SECTION I
Prior to Training

1

Beginnings

"Welcome to Dog Training 101!"

Those are routinely my opening words to first-week classes. Admittedly, it's not all that profound a greeting, but deep and complex isn't the intent. On the contrary, the twofold purpose is to secure relaxed interest and to set the tone. Indeed, the time has come for some serious dog training, but that doesn't imply that handlers must park their senses of empathy and humor at the door.

Owner perspective can become distorted during this sort of schooling. While the following first-meeting remarks aren't verbatim—I don't teach from a script—they're close.

Before getting under way, we need to visit for a moment about perspective—yours. You know why you're here today, yes? To learn how to train your dog, at least according to the gospel of training methods as interpreted by me. Sure. But consider the situation from your pet's point of view. He hasn't a clue about what's going on. How could he? For all he knows, today's gathering is little different from just another trip to the vet.

Now, one element must be acknowledged from the start. This is a dog you're dealing with—not a child. I know that belabors the obvious, but I also know that after a few lessons, students often comment about similarities between teaching the youngster and training the dog. While I grant you that some analogies can be drawn, one does his or her pet a disservice to equate the animal with a human. Dogs can't handle the pressure typically generated by unrealistic anticipations accompanying such a mind-set. There's no way a canine can live up to such expectations, and he finds himself in an impossible, hopeless situation.*

Rather than compare your pet, endeavor to see him for what he is, not for what he isn't. To ignore or gloss over this point is to deny his identity. It can set the animal up for a lifetime of frustration and rejection; it can damage spirit and hamper sincere attempts at bonding. A dog trapped in such a situation will always sense that the owner is less than satisfied with him. What he'll never be able to fathom is why.

Be careful, too, about getting overly wrapped up in training for its own sake. One can become so fascinated with technique and theory as to dwell on ''what'' instead of ''who.'' A dog can come to be seen as an object, a thing, an ego-stroking means to an end, instead of the caring, loyal spirit he is.

A final point pertains to force. Its judicious use is integral to training, but it's not an end in itself. Unawareness of that distinction has led many would-be trainers to evolve into little more than force-oriented controllers knowing just enough to be dangerous. Good people can become such hard-hearted disciples of force methods that they forget why they got a dog in the first place. More than one otherwise rational person has made this slip. In doing so, one loses balance and perspective and defeats the intent of sharing his or her days with a willing, dedicated companion.

Be alert, be wary and be careful.

Like I said: Perspective. Hang on to it.

Lassie, Rin-Tin-Tin, *et al.*

When you see the phrase ''trained dog,'' what thought arises? To my mind, such an animal is one that is reliable in all likely situations. His responses are predictable over a broad range of circumstances. Hearing-assist dogs, seeing eyes, canines in police or military service, herding dogs, circus performers and some competition animals belong in this category.

Notice, though, the phrase is not *well*-trained dog. That's redundant. Canine makeup is such that an animal is either reliable (trained) or he's not (untrained). A dog's perception and behavior are absolute: Do or do

---

*Johannes Grewe wrote in *Deutsche Schutzhundschule* (Denver: Quality Press, 1981), pg. 3: ''Sometimes dogs are shown a kind of love which can only exist between two people and then only because it is based on moral values and is rooted in deep human convictions. This type of love, if offered to dogs, is certainly well-intentioned; however it is not only misplaced, but it may make the dog's life a veritable 'hell on earth' because such sentiments foster keeping practices which are inappropriate for the species.''

not, approach or avoid, yes or no, obey or disregard. This aspect of our best friend leads professionals to agree that half-trained is untrained.

Does this mean a trained dog bats a thousand? Of course not. No being has that faculty. But in many ways a trained canine comes closer to working perfection than you or I, and his off days are fewer and farther apart.

And by the way, keep in mind that Lassie, Rinty and the rest were allowed retakes.

Background—The Pack Concept

Canis familiaris is a semidomesticated pack animal whose nature is to submit to those he perceives as dominant. In turn, he attempts to dominate those he senses are submissive. He doesn't choose this attitude. It's chosen for him; he's driven toward it. The drive operates to ensure survival through and within pack preservation, the continued solidarity of which is integral to each member's existence.

Each pack has a structured leadership hierarchy. At the pinnacle is *Alpha*, the *pack leader*. This animal's will is law. To become your dog's leader, dominance must be secured by demonstrating that there's no need to apply for the Alpha position, as that job's been filled: By you.

To state all this another way, what you call a family, your dog calls a pack. If you permit him to run you, he will. If he sees you as dominant, he'll accept your self-proclaimed status. It's no more complicated than that.

A Logical Consequence

A realistic training approach shows a dog that certain acts are his contribution—his responsibility—to pack well-being. This type of contact makes sense to a dog; it speaks to him; it's communication at *his* level of understanding. To accomplish anything beyond rudimentary conditioning, instruction must match the *dog's* perception of reality: He's the student.

Don't presume a canine can be brought to our world. That's simply not in the cards. A dog will always be a dog. No style of training changes pooch into some offbeat form of *Homo sapiens* (and I wouldn't have it any other way). Our attempt is to relate with a being that possesses neither capacity for speech nor imbued comprehension of the King's English. A dog can learn to connect certain sounds (commands, praise, etc.) with actions on his part, but he can never comprehend the subtle nuances of the spoken word as you and I. Tone of voice and body language are much more conducive to canine understanding.

Learning and Retention Abilities

The dog is a quick learner, and his memory is long; both traits must serve unerringly for life. He has evolved from a violent world characterized by ruthless competition in which one may receive but a single opportunity to learn any fact of life. Dogs instinctively know that woe be unto any animal that forgets a lesson: Such could be that critter's undoing.

For a vivid description of the society from which the dog's ancestors came, ponder Jim Harrison's symbolic representation of the wild kingdom.

In northern Manitoba a man saw a great bald eagle–hanging from its neck, teeth locked in skin and feathers, the bleached skull of a weasel.*

Your pet, which is perhaps peacefully asleep at your feet, may not appear to remember these roots to his past, but be assured they are a part of him, and he of them.

Motivation

Canines appraise situations and events according to whether or not each is personally advantageous. That may seem selfish, but in truth it's survival. Certainty is the goal, the key, because our dogs' world is shaded in very few grays. Its members avoid vague circumstances whenever possible, since nondistinct areas produce anxiety born of uncertainty.

A person's decision to train his or her dog is an exercise in common sense. Implementing that decision is an act of kindness. It provides the basis for an ever-deepening relationship. The dog is afforded the sense of certainty he craves through clear guidelines to live by, and the owner can establish necessary control through rapport-based communication.

Rapport

Rapport is both the means and the end, the seed and the flower. A dog can be multititled, but lacking affinity for the owner, such honors

*From Jim Harrison's "A Year's Changes," from the *Locations* collection (New York: W. W. Norton and Co., 1968).

A Miniature Dachshund named Christie, the author and rapport.

mean little. Rapport is a mind-set, or—if you will—a heart-set. It's an attitude, an atmosphere, an act of faith. I've heard it referred to as expanded consciousness. It may indeed be so. It's certainly a higher level of communication than that governed solely by the world of mechanical collars, force and ritualized, unfelt praise.

Equipment is necessary to initiate and—to a degree—perpetuate the process, but dependence on devices and perceiving them as ends in and of themselves is not only self-limiting; it's unhealthy. Ongoing reliance on gadgetry can block development of friendship and bonding. Your attraction to your dog, properly communicated, ultimately becomes the basis for his attraction to you. This attraction, in turn, becomes the cornerstone of your pet's obedience, his reliability.

It must be understood that the concept of rapport-based training doesn't imply a rose-colored-glasses view that a canine should be coddled, begged or cajoled. The correct inference is that each animal must be spoken to according to his essence. With a mild-tempered dog, very little compulsion is needed. With a supertough animal, a sterner approach is appropriate. This is a conceptual expansion of working with each dog at that animal's level of understanding. Moreover, it is not the trainer but the dog that sets the degree of force required. The trainer merely reacts to the dog.

Attitudes and Perceptions

Of a trainer's three primary assets—sincerity, a sense of humor and open-mindedness—sincerity tops the list. Adopting a front risks missing out on much. Dogs recognize artificial behavior in a blink, and a false face creates distance. Canines are uncomfortable in the presence of the unnatural and the unreal. Phoniness is not of their world because posturing is unreal by definition. It's an illusion. A patronizing manner belies and insults a dog's natural openness and conflicts with the animal's inherent freeness of spirit. Since communication must occur in a manner a canine can understand, a trainer's persona must parallel the dog's inborn tendencies to be honest, straightforward, open and positive. Teaching in a responsible, secure and positive manner results in a reliable, confident, happy worker. If training occurs from a negative, overbearing and contrived stance, confusion and isolation are the almost certain result.

Trait number two—a sense of humor—keeps perspective alive (and sanity intact). Without it, capacities for forgiveness and learning are severely handicapped. Openness goes out the window. One becomes unable to distinguish between such disparate behaviors as out-and-out disobedience and simple insecurity. An overly stern, inflexible individual can actually place a psychic barrier between himself and pooch without being aware of having done so.

The third element, open-mindedness, facilitates the other two. Trainers can't afford the lofty luxury of forsaking a "Well, I'll be!" attitude in the face of effective new approaches and methods. Consider those who've been in the business for, say, twenty years and haven't discovered anything new in the past nineteen. Those folks were blessed with the miraculous good fortune of achieving mastery in a few months. They paid a dear price, though—they forgot that learning is a lifelong process of discovery.

> In the beginner's mind there are many possibilities; in the expert's mind there are few.*

To be sure, professionals can make it look easy. Some folks in any craft develop a touch for their work. However, an unspoken truth is that the pro has learned it *is* easy to deal with members of a species that, for the most part, are quite content to be dealt with. Canine willingness to be led and to revel in human companionship constitutes much of their attraction for us in the first place, giving rise to expressions like "man's best friend." Were this untrue, dogs wouldn't occupy the special place in our hearts they do. These unique traits are large plusses that fledgling trainers—and experienced ones—sometimes overlook.

It's a Two-Way Street

The assumption that only trainers may teach and only dogs may learn is not only faulty but dangerous thinking. It's egocentricity that's both limiting and ironic. Canine training is establishing communication between two species. You're perusing this text for knowledge to accomplish that laudable end. The irony is that your dog already knows how. He was born with an instinct to accede to a pack leader's wishes.

> A dog will readily, and happily, comply with any reasonable request. He usually knows already how to do it. The trainer, however, must formulate the request in a manner that is understood by the dog.**

*From *Zen Mind, Beginner's Mind*, by Shunryu Suzuki, as quoted in *Journey of Awakening*, by Ram Dass, (New York: Bantam Books, 1978), p. 11.
**Dietmar Schellenberg, *Top Working Dogs—A Training Manual* (Webster, N.Y.: D.C.B. Publishing, 1985), p. 3.

A sound animal is responsive to sincere human attempts at interaction. What you must develop is communicative skills styled so pooch can understand them. In a phrase, you need to learn to "think dog." This book can teach you how, and if you listen to your pet's feedback, so can he.

There's no magic in dog training, nor is much about the art chiseled in stone. Moreover, training is far more art than science. Methods can be outlined with a degree of exactitude, but the application of technique is an art that varies from dog to dog. Training denotes entry into another realm, a dimension having few hard-and-fast rules. True, the dog's sphere is absolute, but that doesn't imply that your perceptions must be rigid or autocratic.

The Proverbial Bottom Line

"But I've never trained a dog—how much can I accomplish?"

Dog training is seldom difficult or complex. Stated colloquially, it's often a good deal of work, but it's not that hard.

> With enough practice . . . [these] skills will become second nature and your feelings of awkwardness will lessen. They will become part of your humanity rather than something tacked onto it.*

Dr. Egan was writing about human therapeutic counseling, but his words are certainly germane. Your dog's willingness and your own good intentions and determination will usher you past many seeming barriers. Even if you only teach Sit, expect police-dog reliability. It's highly probable that your pooch has the potential for such dependability and that you're capable of that caliber of training.

Reflection

> In the beginning, God created man, but seeing him so feeble, He gave him the dog.
>
> Toussenel

---

*Gerard Egan, *The Skilled Helper*, (Pacific Grove, Calif.: Brooks/Cole Publishing Co., 1986), p. 58.

10

2

The Right Dog

PLEASE DO yourself a favor: Start with the right canine. The animal need not be the biggest, the littlest, the cutest, the friendliest, the toughest, the most expensive or the ''best'' dog (whatever that might be), but make sure he's right for your purposes. You'll save yourself much grief down the road.

A reality of professional dog training is that instructors universally agree on few teaching principles. Most questions elicit as many shades of answers as the number of trainers asked. The more general the questions, the more variance in the answers (all of which will be ''right,'' incidentally, *from each particular trainer's perspective*—as mentioned earlier, training is an art). Among professionals, however, I've yet to discern sentiment contrary to starting with the ''right dog'' for the tasks at hand.

You needn't attempt to seek out the ''perfect'' animal, but training goals must be reasonable for each particular breed. The Bloodhound isn't the obedience candidate that the Doberman Pinscher is, but the Bloodhound leaves the Dobie far behind in tracking ability. Neither can compete at herding with a Belgian Tervuren, and none of the three can compare with a Yorkshire Terrier as a lapdog.

Think of it this way: The first rule of training is: Start with the right dog. The second rule is: Don't try to get around the first rule. One doesn't obtain a West Highland White to race with Greyhounds (though don't ever tell a Westie that). No breed is inherently better than another, but certain breeds are better suited to your particular situation and desires than others.

SELECTION FACTORS

Small, Medium, Large, or Omigod!

Several variables determine what constitutes the right dog for you. Probably the first is size. Do you want a huge animal, a tiny one or one somewhere in between? Consider each breed's food requirements (as well as cleanups), their needs for exercise, your life-style, home conditions and physical and emotional attributes.

With respect to size and strength, ascribe to a single rule: Don't acquire a canine you can't easily control physically in any situation when the animal is full grown. Some are a powerhouse when the heat's on, and an owner can actually be at risk in high-stress situations.

Fuzzy or Otherwise?

Once you settle on size, coat type and length could well be the next consideration. Coat is an important factor in relation to how and where a dog is housed. Whippets aren't made for harsh winters; Siberian Huskies can be miserable in a warm house. Do you have the time for grooming a long-coated companion, or are you better suited to a shorthaired one?

Purebred Versus Crossbreed; Registered Versus Unpapered

For some, this topic might be first on the list. Do you want a purebred, or might a canine of mixed parentage do? If you settle on a recognized breed, does it matter whether the dog is AKC registerable?

Points to consider are these: With a registered animal, one can select not only breed but bloodlines as well. Some are decidedly stronger in desirable qualities than others. At the same time, purchase of a purebred can wreak havoc on the bank account. Some breeders have whimsical notions about their pup's worth.

Remember, too, if you plan to show in AKC competition, the dog must be registered with that organization. Before any canine can be registered, the animal must first be a member of an AKC-recognized breed.

If you have no interest in showing, perhaps you'd be happy with a mixed breed. Companionship is where you find it, and no correlation exists between canine affection and purebred versus mixed-breed status. Besides, every year a staggering number of unwanted animals whose only crime is mixed parentage are destroyed at dog pounds. The right dog might be waiting for you at the local shelter, where you'll also find many homeless purebreds.

Breed Selection

If you decide on a purebred, be aware of breed tendencies before making a choice. Given the number of breeds in existence, delineating the characteristics and qualities common to each is beyond the scope of a general obedience book. Once you've tentatively selected a breed, seek out people who own such a dog. Ask for impressions of their dogs. What problems have they encountered? What are the breed's strong and weak points? Would they own another of the same breed? Why, or why not? Doubtless you'll notice a commonality among the responses. Then you can decide if the traits mentioned are in line with your needs.

Talk with breeders and study breed books, but in both cases remember that reading between the lines may be necessary. Breeders and breed books promote their dog's positive aspects, understandably. The problem is that a positive trait to one person may be a neutral or even a negative component to another.

Gender

The issue here, of course, is the choice between male and female, or—in the parlance of canine terminology—the choice between dog and bitch. Males of a given breed are usually larger; females are often quicker. A dog will never present you with an unwanted litter, but neither will a bitch if she's spayed or protected during estrus.

Wee Bairn, Teenager or Adult?

Another choice is that between puppy or more mature dog. Do you have the time and patience it takes to rear a pup properly, or would you rather take your chances with an older canine that may harbor effects of former human relationships (or the lack thereof)?

Roles

What purpose will a dog serve in your life? Will he be primarily a house pet? Do you have any interest in competition? Will the animal be a worker, as in herding, protection or hunting? If you have children, will pooch be a part of their lives? All are basic questions that are better contemplated now than after the fact.

I have a male Doberman Pinscher that is as thoroughly trained a canine as it has ever been my privilege and pleasure to know. Were I a hunter, however, though I've no doubt this fine dog would give more than a passing account of himself, he or any other Doberman would not be my first choice as a field companion. The breed just isn't "right" for the work. The typical Pomeranian would make a super guard dog if intelligence, willingness and heart were the sole prerequisites. Size limits the Pom for man work, though. In a real situation, one well-placed kick from a human aggressor and the fight would be over.

Only you can say which breed is right for you. Though if you live in an apartment, are on a limited budget or are more comfortable with a lapdog, dispel any notions of owning a Great Dane, Briard or Borzoi. At the same time, one who aspires to Schutzhund (protection-dog) competition could make a better choice than an Afghan Hound, Saint Bernard, or Brittany.

Sound Temperament: An Essential Quality

Once decisions about breed, gender, age and purpose have been made, the selection process narrows to picking a specific animal. When setting out to acquire a canine, put stable temperament at the top of your criteria list for the right dog. Seek neither a truculent pooch nor one that is excessively soft emotionally. Either can present severe training and bonding difficulties. Likewise, pass on the ultradominant or supersubmissive dog. Extreme personalities often present extreme problems. Stick with middle-of-the-road, positive temperament.

The puppy that shivers in a warm corner and the older dog that often looks sideways at you should hold equal appeal: none whatsoever! These fear-driven animals are best avoided, as are those that exhibit such extreme boldness that they tend to leap before looking. Both often represent genetic aberrations that are accidents waiting for a place to happen. True, the dog didn't choose his genes—it's not as though he made a conscious choice to be the way he is—but realize also that all the well-intended caring in the world cannot reverse or override defective chromosomes.

14

Training won't—can't—change faulty genetics. A genetically unsound canine can never be reliable.

We tend to champion the underdog, and I, too, feel pity for one that just isn't "right." But in all candor I feel a good deal more sympathy for the owner of such an animal. Too many good dogs are looking for homes to waste time and effort on an obvious bad actor. Though no fault of the dog's, the critter is often a heartbreaker. He simply doesn't have what it takes. Moreover, this lack will be most apparent in stressful situations, which is when stability is needed most.

Mentally Disturbed Canines

Through her book *No Bad Dogs*, Barbara Woodhouse fostered the curious notion that no maladaptive canines exist. Except for herself, she did no one a positive service in promoting that fallacious concept. Granted, it's an easy notion to peddle; it's the sort of thing we'd like to believe, notwithstanding the obvious naïveté inherent in such an assertion. A percentage of every species arrives on this earth with less than a full complement of essential attributes.

Dr. Michael Fox concludes, "Symptoms of delinquency and antisocial tendencies, even sociopathic behavior . . . (in dogs) is a reality."*

Dr. Fox's thought is echoed and amplified by Job Michael Evans, who responded to the Woodhouse fable by writing:

> Something should definitely be done to rehabilitate those who breed such specimens, but often they have already gone out of business as soon as the genetic junk they flood the market with has matured into prime biting age. There are bad dogs, so to speak, but anthropomorphic thinking also has to be avoided. The dog itself did not chose to be "bad" and in almost every case, there is an unthinking or just plain stupid human who is ultimately responsible for the situation.**

Understand, I'm attempting neither to scare you nor to recommend a nit-picking approach for selecting a canine friend. Like you and me, they all have their virtues and faults. My twofold purpose is to remind you that whatever animal you settle on is likely going to be with you for at least several years, given the nature of commitment, and that an extremely maladaptive personality will disappoint in the long run.

*Dr. Michael Fox, *Understanding Your Dog* (New York: Coward, McCann and Geoghegan, Inc., 1972), p. 190.
**Job Michael Evans, *The Evans Guide for Counseling Dog Owners*. Section entitled "Are There 'Bad Dogs'?", (New York: Howell Book House, 1985), p. 117.

So how does one with little or no canine experience identify sound temperament? Discerning the quality in an older dog can be tricky. Because the animal has been on the planet longer, the effects of learning can obscure the genetic traits with which he was born. This is true to the extent that when evaluating a mature canine, one must also get a reading on the animal's owner and environment to determine the degree to which each may have influenced the dog.

Various tests have been devised to screen mature canine temperament. While helpful in some cases, such as evaluating a dog for specific training (police or military service, seeing eye, hunting, herding etc.), many are so subjective in interpretation that the results can be colored by tester predispositions and rationalizations.

To evaluate mature canine temperament, plan on spending some time with the animal. A hurried once-over discloses little, but two or three hours around a dog can reveal much. During that length of time, the newness of your arrival wears off and ceases to influence behavior; the dog shows more of himself. Once the animal settles, the simple act of walking away while suggestively patting your leg can locate a potential companion. This is especially true of the pooch that tries to make eye contact as he trots along with you. Both are signals of willingness, an essential quality. It's not that a good dog never resists an owner's overtures, but some make a career of it. It's self-evident that recalcitrant animals require far more time and effort than stable ones while yielding fractional results. Few dogs make up this category of losers: those that dispute trainer intent every step of the way and those having such extremely soft temperaments that every waking moment is a study in terror. Either extreme is best avoided.

Finally, review the following material on puppy testing. Much of the information applies to mature dogs as well as to young ones.

GROUP TEMPERAMENT TESTING—PUPPIES

Picking one puppy from among a herd of adorable fuzzballs can be difficult. Pups are endearing, and thoughts of "I wish I could take them all home" come to mind. Reason usually prevails, though, with the concession that each puppy will one day be a grown dog. Evaluating a mature animal seems simple by comparison, if for no other reason than the heartstrings aren't tugged quite so much. But how does one choose *the* puppy?

Formal temperament tests, such as those established by the American Temperament Testing Society (which are included in many breed

Eight-week-old Doberman Pinscher puppies exhibiting a wide range of temperaments and attitudes.

books), are conducted with one pup at a time. However, some studies can involve the litter as a whole. While many are similar in nature to the formal exams, they're less definitive because the support each puppy draws from the litter can mask traits. Still, group tests are helpful as overall temperament indicators and can be made in any familiar setting as soon as the young ones are old enough to walk and puppy-run.

Physical Fitness

The first element relates to health. Is each of the pups eating and drinking normally, and is each putting on weight in proportion to ingestion rate and skeletal structure? Should a pup appear generally listless and be constantly disinterested in food, a trip to the vet is warranted. If no medical problem is discerned, a temperament weakness may be operating. While not absolute, experience suggests that the puppy that cares little for sustenance—especially with the nearby stimulus of the litter taking its food heartily—won't have much interest in learning. When motivation toward life's basics is missing, there's scant inducement an owner can offer to promote bonding.

Sociability

How well does each puppy get along with his or her littermates? The animal that is constantly squabbling is as worrisome as the pup that is always withdrawn. Neither is suitable for homes where other animals or children are present, the former for obvious reasons and the latter because the dog may develop into a fear biter (a canine that reflexively responds with aggression to normal contact situations).

To emphasize an earlier point, watch for extreme behavior patterns, not merely slight or infrequent exaggerations. Some pups are more rowdy than the norm, while others are more reserved. Either condition is acceptable. Unending, neck-ripping aggression is not, nor is constant apathy.

Playfulness

Note which pups enjoy play versus those that are uninterested in fun and frolic. The young dog that seldom participates may harbor a temperament weakness—playfulness is a normal puppy drive. Also, remember there's a difference between a playful pup and one that seeks only to control. Some young dogs will manifest excessively dominant tendencies through despotic behaviors. Superficially their actions may appear playful, but studied observation may reveal that dictatorial tendencies are the actual driving force.

Intelligence

In any litter, some members are brighter than others. Don't be concerned if one or more of the pups is a trifle slow—the key is that the young animal tries to learn. If it takes him or her a little longer to grasp certain lessons, so what? Perseverance is what matters. The pup that shows no interest in acquiring knowledge is the one with problems.

Cleanliness

Another temperature barometer is a puppy's attitude toward cleanliness. That's not to suggest concern if he or she delights in playing in mud. Puppies do that sort of thing for a living. However, it is distressing should a pup sleep atop droppings or habitually ingest them. At the very least, the animal may prove difficult, if not impossible, to housebreak. For a puppy to run through an unnoticed pile is neither unusual nor alarming. For a pup to live in a world of attraction toward filth is unacceptable.

A related consideration is the location where puppy often seeks relief. The pup that frequently evacuates two inches from the sleep area or food dish is less desirable than one that moves several feet away from these sites prior to letting go.

Group Play

The simple act of rolling a ball in the litter's midst can indicate individual degrees of play and prey drives as well as dominant versus submissive tendencies. It's also a good locator of retrieving and protection candidates. The pup that shows little interest isn't necessarily a potential problem—he or she might be perfect for someone with a less than active life-style. It's the pup that responds with fear toward the toy's motion that is abnormal.

Older Canines

How a puppy responds to older dogs is an indicator of how he'll relate to humans. This is because in both situations the key is social behavior. If you have a mature dog you can trust not to maul the little ones, escort the animal to the litter area and note the pups' reactions.

Again, watch for extreme responses. The pup that takes one bug-eyed look and flees at full yelp with tucked tail displays abnormal behavior. So does the one that immediately launches an all-out attack toward the visitor. Either pup is unsuitable for homes with other animals or children.

Human Attraction

Friendly visitors appearing on the scene and walking among the litter can identify those drawn to human companionship. Most puppies will approach out of curiosity. Those that come near and remain are people pups; those that immediately vacate the area in favor of a hiding place aren't. However, pups that go bouncing off in favor of other activities aren't necessarily loners. More than likely they were simply distracted for the moment. Puppies are like that.

Strangers

Observe how the pups respond to strangers. The young ones should exhibit curiosity and varying degrees of dominant and submissive behaviors. Should one or two of the young ones show little interest toward a newcomer, note the reaction but don't lose sleep over it. Unless a pup displays chronic fear reactions to the presence of strangers, just remember that some canines are more aloof than others. Should an entire litter appear uninterested—moreover, should they run from an individual—the problem is likely the person, not the pups.

Petting and Holding

The puppy that dislikes being petted isn't companion material. This is especially true of the pup that responds with a sideways, lowered-head look as he slinks away. If the response is playful or even mildly aggressive, however, the pup is fine as long as the prospective owner is an active individual.

A similar test is simply picking up a puppy. Affection, relaxed acceptance or mild fidgeting are acceptable responses; hysterical struggling or fearful shaking or biting aren't.

Sudden Noise

Puppy reactions to the sound of a sealed tin can containing a few pebbles dropped unseen a few feet from the litter is a good indicator of stability. Some pups will mildly flinch; others won't show much reaction. Either response is acceptable. The problem puppy will display a pronounced startled response and will either remain frozen in place, perhaps shaking in fear, or may instantly flee the area before the object comes to rest. Of equal concern is the puppy that blindly attacks the object. Either reaction indicates unstable temperament and is suggestive of a potential fear biter.

Curiosity and Spirit

Look for curiosity in a young dog. Does he explore the new and unknown, or does he seem uninterested or even intimidated by things new to his world? Evaluate the quality of spirit, the sense of élan, the self-esteem. Admittedly, these are smoky, nebulous concepts that don't easily lend themselves to quantitative analysis. Though something of a paradox, it's sometimes harder to define the positive aspects or qualities present in the puppy that feels good about himself than it is to identify negatives in one that has a poor sense of self-worth, that suffers from the "plastered-tail syndrome." The latter looks at people without turning or raising his head, which he often holds down. His opposite number only puts his head down for a purpose, such as eating, scenting or playing.

Touch Sensitivity

Subject the animal that seems to be the companion you're seeking to one final test. Using the fleshy part of thumb and finger—*not* the fingernails—slowly compress the webbing between any of the front toes, counting from one to ten while steadily increasing pressure. The test is completed (i.e., *pressure must instantly stop*) as soon as the dog shows *any* discomfort, such as whining or attempting to pull the foot away.

Extreme readings at either end of the scale indicate an animal that may be difficult to train. The pooch that withdraws the foot at the first hint of pressure won't be able to emotionally handle corrections (physical discipline); the one that merely yawns as the count is completed likely wouldn't notice them.

Take care not to be bitten when applying the test to an older canine. It's unlikely that a dog that has passed the other exams would respond with aggression, but the possibility exists. Furthermore, don't bother with this test if the animal hasn't done well so far. Whether testing a puppy or a mature dog, follow the test with petting to show you aren't trying to make an enemy.

THE LEGACY OF OLD BUSTER

Ponder the relationship between the concept of the "right dog" and the characterization of "Old Buster."

He was just the best dog you ever did see, Old Buster was. Never had a moment's bother with him. You'd tell him to hush up or to go and lay down, and he'd do it right now. Never had no training or nothing. Didn't seem to need none. You'd just show him something and he'd do it, that's all.

He was real good with the kids, too. Even when they'd pull on his ears and such, he'd never snap at them or nothing. Never messed in the house even once and never jumped up on nobody, neither. He was a good dog, Old Buster was.

Many of us have fond memories of "Old Buster." I've had the good fortune to meet this noble dog; perhaps so have you. The drawback to having known such a fine animal is that an owner's perception of every canine encountered thereafter can be colored by Old Buster's memory. No other dog can measure up to what he was or fill the void left in the lives of those he touched.

If you've ever been blessed with such a pet, be thankful for the joy and warmth he brought you but avoid cheapening the dog's memory by judging others against him. To do so places your present companion in a futile, stacked-deck situation, one in which he can't possibly shine.

I've known people who owned the right dog but couldn't see the animal for what he was. They were held captive by remembrances of Old Buster. Old B. deserves a better epitaph, and your here-and-now companion merits a more compassionate welcome.

Reflection

God made the earth, the sky and the water, the moon and the sun. He made man and bird and beast. But He didn't make the dog: He already had one.

American Indian saying, quoted by Bill Tarrant in
The Best Way to Train Your Gun Dog

3

Pretraining and Bonding

$\mathbf{M}$OST OF THE FOLLOWING applies evenly to puppies and to older dogs. Notes accompany exceptions unless the distinction is obvious, such as material on teething, puppy classes and so forth.

Training Age

People inquiring about my training services ask one question more than any other: When is the dog old enough to train? The correct time is when pooch can handle concomitant stress. This is generally between six to eight months. Now, before chiseling that statistic into granite, consider the following qualifiers and explanations.

The training referred to is formal obedience. Basic manners (housebreaking, learning not to vanquish the family cat etc.) can be taught at two to four months, depending on maturation. When advising clients to delay initiation of formal obedience until their pets are at least six months old, responses range from "Okay" to "Oh, my God! I don't know if I can endure this character's antics until then." With the larger breeds, holding off on training may create some temporary problems, but not so many as can arise from starting too soon. Puppies pass through a series of highly impressionable phases, usually referred to as the *critical periods*. During these intervals, a dog prematurely started in obedience can easily form negative attitudes toward a leash, a collar or even toward the owner.

Without getting into all the ramifications of this phenomenon, suffice it to say that a puppy can easily adopt a predisposition toward fear during this time. Once internalized, such phobias are difficult, if not impossible, to alleviate later.

> It is important to remember that while previous learning may be altered by subsequent learning, subsequent learning will never obliterate previous learning.*

Until the young one shows some maturity—such as a lengthened attention span—allow the puppy to be a puppy.

Age Is a Relative Concept

Thus far the discussion has centered on chronological age, but there's a second perspective from which to view the question, "How old should my pet be to begin serious training?" The three-year-old pooch acquired this afternoon is still a bit too young. A canine freshly arrived in a new home must have time to settle in. He needs a few days to acclimate to the new surroundings, to develop senses of trust and belonging, before training can be introduced without risking undue stress. Remember, change precipitates anxiety in a dog, and it's unwise to subject a strained animal to a second stressful situation.

Experienced trainers often allow two to five days for acclimation prior to commencing obedience. Specifically, most wait until the animal is eating and eliminating normally and seems generally at ease. If your experience with dogs is limited, delay any formal work for at least a week after obtaining a new animal that is otherwise old enough. This interval affords the novice an adequate safety net of time should he or she unknowingly have a dog that needs more than the usual two- to five-day adjustment period. The "If in doubt, don't" principle applies. It's safer to wait longer than might be really needed than it is to chance long-term damaging effects from starting prematurely.

Breed and Gender Influences

Two other considerations governing when to begin training are breed and gender. As a rule, the larger the breed, the slower the rate of emotional

*J. Paul Scott, Ph.D., as quoted by Clarance Pfaffenberger in *The New Knowledge of Dog Behavior* (New York: Howell Book House Inc., 1963), p. 132. This book is an excellent source for further information about the critical periods.

maturation. Thus, the bigger the dog, the later an obedience program should be started. A client once observed that such a seemingly contradictory status was "a cruel joke by the Gods." She stated a valid point: The larger the dog, the sooner the owner needs control, sometimes rather desperately. The frustration of an inexperienced owner of a large, unruly pup is understandable, but much is risked by commencing too soon.

Regarding gender, males often mature more slowly than females of the same breed. A young female can usually be started in formal obedience sooner than can a male of the same age and breed. This isn't an absolute rule—very few of those exist in training—but it's a tendency more often than not.

Health and History

Don't begin training if pooch is ill or harboring a parasitic infestation. I state this obvious point only because some curious types feel that "he'll come around after a little work." One need not be a professional trainer to realize that any illness is stressful by definition and that the last thing an already weakened organism needs is more pressure.

On the subject of history, mentally categorize your dog's past as healthy or unhealthy. The animal that has had a compassionate upbringing can be started as soon as the other factors mentioned are in line. The pooch that has had a tough time—that is, one that was a victim of abuse or neglect—needs a longer adaptation period before training should start.

Working with Abused Dogs

The biggest single kindness you can bestow on an abused canine—beyond giving him a good home—is to treat the animal according to his essence. Relate to him based on what he is deep inside, not in terms of where he's been. If one pampers, babies and otherwise handles such an animal extraordinarily, he's being treated *like an abused dog*. True, that's what he *was*, but starting from the time he came to your home, he no longer was.

A dog that has gone through sad times should be loved but not coddled, accepted but not fawned over. He should be given a sense of belonging but not of dominating the homestead. While you'll be mindful of his past, your relationship with the animal must concern itself with today and tomorrow. To relate differently than you would with a normally raised canine is—in a very real sense—to perpetuate the abuse process. It exchanges one form of extreme human behavior for another, the end result being a stifling environment in which no animal can grow and flourish. If you hang on to his past, so must he. Let it go and give him room to breathe.

A specific technique for releasing a dog from past fears is renaming the animal once he's in a new home. The sound of an old name can trigger old memories. A new name makes it possible to start fresh. To change a dog's name, merely begin using the new one. He'll quickly catch on. Don't fall for the fuzzy logic of using the old name and the new one together, dropping the former over time. Some think that's the best way to make a dog see what the new name represents. In truth, however, all the method does is link the old appellation with the new one. Such a dog desperately needs to shed his past, and renaming is one of the quicker ways to help him accomplish that end. Otherwise, every time he hears the old name, he can "hear" old fears.

Trainer/Trainee Relationship

Two final factors in the equation of when to begin lessons relate to the trainer. First, as a dog must have time to adapt to a new home, you must have sufficient time to get to know your pet. Unless you make your living with canines (and sometimes even then), pooch will figure you out a lot quicker than you will him. So even if the animal seems ready, make sure you're comfortable in your assessment of him. Each is a bit different, and some are more difficult to read than others. Until you have some valid clues about his makeup and until some glimmer of contact has occurred between you (even if only at feeding time), don't initiate training.

Second, be aware that with some canines the possibility for a gender conflict between you (or your spouse) and the dog can exist. Some animals not only prefer the company of a woman over a man, or vice versa, but simply won't initially tolerate being commanded by one over the other. It's not so much a matter of the dog "liking" one person more than the other but of feeling more of a sense of identity with one individual. This tendency is often genetically based and can be reinforced by learning.

In such a situation, especially when a husband-wife team is involved with their pet's training, follow the path of deflection: Have the person the dog prefers start the training, with the thought that the other individual can ease into the picture after specific learning has occurred. This approach lowers the rate of contention and resentment.

A conflicting school of thought holds that it's better to meet such resistance head-on through confrontation by the trainer, with whom the animal is less at ease. The purpose is to say to the dog that he must be obedient regardless of predispositions. While it's true that he must, it's fairer to hold him accountable only after he's been trained to some degree and understands the ground rules. To force a confrontation sooner is not only premature; it's uncalled for. Once the lessons are well under way the other person can enter the picture, but it's nonsense to facilitate trouble at the onset. To do so creates a confrontational situation that might never have existed otherwise.

When Not to Commence Training

It's unwise to initiate training following any stressful period, such as neutering, being boarded for the first time, moving, illness, injury, breeding, family unrest or a heat cycle (especially the first one).

Should your female come into season during training, hang up the leash for a few weeks. Solitaire, my first Doberman, was in her second estrus when she demonstrated this point so well. She knew advanced obedience and was reliable off leash among heavy distractions. While playing ball with her one day, I commanded Sol to the Heel position in preparation for a retrieve. She responded with her characteristic Flip Finish—whereby a dog hops from a position of sitting in front of the trainer to sitting at his or her left side, facing forward—winding up in as straight a Sit as one could ask for. The only problem was that she alighted at my right side (instead of at my left, as she'd been trained) and facing in the wrong direction: Backward. I'll never forget her beaming expression of pride and confidence, totally convinced she had performed with precision and exactitude.

Continued practice could easily have caused faulty learning. Had she been commanded to Finish several more times and had she responded as before, the animal could have learned that her incorrect response was indeed correct. Later eradication would have been difficult at best. By the way, no, I didn't chastise her. A trainer doesn't correct a confused animal or one that is trying to do his or her level best. I simply sighed, "Very nice, Solitaire. Let's play ball some more," which she thought was a dandy idea. I also muttered, as much to myself as to the Doberman, "Thanks for the reminder."

Foundational Training and the Playtoy

Once a pup shows interest in a piece of burlap being pulled teasingly away or a ball being rolled across the ground, it's time to begin retrieving and/or protection play-work. If the mature animal you recently acquired hasn't experienced this type of play training, don't be surprised if he reacts to games in puppylike fashion. He'll display more pronounced quickness and coordination than a pup would, of course, but his antics may still seem immature. Such actions tell you there haven't been previous opportunities to ventilate puppyish enthusiasm. However, you'll also see that the older canine passes through this stage much more quickly than would a pup.

Tennis balls serve well as play toys, owing to their low cost and the fact that should the object take a strange bounce and hit the dog, it's less likely to startle the animal. If you think your pal would enjoy games of tug-of-war, use washed burlap sacks* rather than towels for play purposes so as not to teach pooch to consume the laundry. If your pet responds with interest to the game, make certain he always wins (achieves possession of the sack). To allow him to lose could not only lessen enthusiasm; it could teach that he should expect to lose from time to time. While that may be a realistic lesson for a human, it's inappropriate in the world of canines. The dog that tastes defeat often learns hesitation and develops a lack of self-confidence. Remember, dogs live in a world of absolutes, and experience with losing inserts a "maybe" into the psyche of an animal not structured to deal with such uncertainty.

Along this same vein, don't teach a canine—whether a puppy or mature dog—to "Let go!" until he's had much experience with victory. Doing so risks dampening ardor for the game, attraction to the play object or trust in you. (To end playtime, either wait until pooch drops the toy and lead him away or pull the object from his mouth, but don't pressure the animal to effect a release.) If a novice dog is forced to release an article, he can learn to relate nervousness with the activity. He may begin to focus on the anticipated "Let go!" and the pressure associated with it. The effect of such stressful learning is to distract from the joy of the game, which defeats the purpose. Not only can untimely force teach a premature release, but a dog can even learn that he's better off not mouthing the object at all. This attitude can later haunt a trainer when trying to teach retrieving or protection.

Whatever toy you prefer, hide it away once playtime is over. If it's left to lie about, attraction to it lessens markedly—the animal comes to take it for granted—thereby diminishing the toy's effectiveness. It's to appear only when you do, and then only sometimes. The idea is for pooch to associate the pleasurable object with you.

---

*The "washed" stipulation is to make sure the burlap harbors no residual insecticide, which is often the case with sacks used to transport crops.

Building the retrieving habit in a Doberman pup. He's already learned that it's fun to chase an object and that the only way he can pursue it is by bringing it to the trainer so it can be thrown again. A good deal of foundational training can precede formal instruction.

The few rules governing the proper use of play articles come under the heading "The Dog Cannot Do Anything Wrong with a Play Toy." That is, if he's interested in the thrown ball, fine. Should he give chase and pounce on it, fine. If he picks it up and runs away with it, fine. If he relieves himself on it, fine. Pooch can't do anything improper with a play toy—it's just not possible. Sending any negative messages that a canine could infer as relating to the play object can easily lessen attraction to the article.

To instill and heighten interest in a play toy, begin by kneeling next to the dog. (The dominating pressure imparted by human body language when standing over a canine can distract from the moment—in general, things above a dog seize his attention.) Roll the ball back and forth between your hands, staring pointedly at the object while observing your companion's reactions peripherally. As interest develops, swiftly move the article to the side of your leg, causing pooch to search for the toy. As fascination increases, allow the dog to pounce on and carry off the object to the accompaniment of your expressed approval.

The purpose is to tempt the animal with a play toy until he displays strong attraction to it. Making capture of an article too easy can cause lost interest for want of challenge and stimulation. At the same time, don't prolong teasing to the extent that desire wanes. That could teach a losing attitude.

When playing with very young or inexperienced animals, roll the ball rather than throwing it. Until a young dog has had some practice in pursuing an object, he's unable to follow visually the flight of a thrown ball* and can easily become confused or frustrated to the extent of losing interest. Field and depth of vision expand with maturity.

If you're working with several puppies, merely dropping a play toy in their vicinity creates much enticement. (Don't try this with mature dogs—doing so could trigger a battle.) Invariably, one pup will grab the object, if for no other reason than to prevent another from doing so, and the game is begun. If you have an older animal that enjoys chasing a ball, allow the pups to watch from a respectful, safe distance, preferably from behind a fence so they can't interfere with the activity and/or perhaps be snapped at. The idea is to stimulate interest and heighten their drive to participate.

---

*Very young canines are normally nearsighted. This is a survival mechanism, as puppies could otherwise be visually drawn from the protection of the nest toward situations that could prove life threatening.

Praise

When pooch does something that pleases you, tell him. Share that approval. For example, when the animal trots back to you with *his* ball, pet and praise repetitively, saying, "Good Bring." Don't be in a hurry to take the object, lest the dog learn to come with his head lowered (to make taking the toy harder) or to not come at all. When you do take the article, immediately throw it again. Don't tease excessively first—take the toy, wave it in front of the dog's nose a time or two and throw it. Canines enjoy pursuit as much as they do possession. The purposes are to show your pet that it's in his interests to release the toy to you and to keep his eyes on you afterward.

When petting a dog, especially one with erect ears, confine the fondling to the underside of neck and muzzle. The idea is to teach your pet to look up at you. Petting atop the head can easily appear to be a push-away signal—look at the gesture from the dog's perspective—but stroking under the jaw invites looking upward, toward the source. This manner of touching is expressly important with regard to outsiders you allow to pet your animal. Petting atop the head can cause a canine to not only lower it but to pull down or flatten his ears submissively, and it's unwise to suggest a mind-set of automatic submission toward strangers. Friendliness and curiosity, yes; submission, no.

Unintended Lessons

Consider the following example of subtle training that can take place inadvertently: While reassurance can be helpful with children, it's a sure way to cause apprehension and anxiety in a dog. For instance, should a sudden sound cause your friend to startle, ignore both the noise and his anxiety. Rushing to him with "It's all right. Don't worry" and so forth may only reinforce the nervous reaction to sudden noises. Yes, pet him as you normally would if he comes to you, but no, don't fly to him with the express purpose of reassurance. Consider: Canines have no built-in fear of thunder—it's a natural phenomenon, and dogs are beings of nature—but many owners have educated their pets to fear such loud noises. A dog's reaction to pointless reassurance is "If everything's so fine and dandy, then just what are *you* so concerned about?" If a given sound doesn't worry you, don't teach your pet to fear it.

You're Always Onstage

Similarly, remember that whenever you're near your companion, even if you aren't actively engaged with him at the moment, you are in fact teaching the animal, whether you mean to be or not.

Collars

Regardless of your type of collar preference, *be sure* to remove it when you aren't going to be nearby for a while—even for a few minutes! A curious, adventuresome puppy or older dog can discover myriad ways of catching a collar on something. Such happenings are usually traumatic and can easily be fatal.

Identifiers

Assign names to things for your pal. In addition to their command vocabularies, my dogs have an understanding of objects and concepts numbering another forty-plus terms. Some handy words are *outside, yard, car, truck, house, chair, couch, bed, nest,* (food) *dish, dinner* (feeding time), *drink, ball, lead, collar, sack* (burlap), *rabbit, horse, bird, critter* (bovine), *deer, warm* and *cold.* Saying the word a few times when the animal happens to focus attention on the object or condition sends the message.

Puppy Classes

I've mixed feelings about the concept of puppy classes. They're fine as a socialization vehicle, but that potential is offset by their inherent risk of spreading disease. Also, unless the instructor is experienced, knowledgeable and skilled, the puppy's psyche can be at risk.

From a training standpoint, such classes can be detrimental to long-range goals. For instance, in many classes a puppy is taught that he may ignore the command to Sit (for example), as no serious force is used to back up the command. The trouble is that "Sit," like any other command, says, "Do this thing until you're told to do something else." It doesn't mean "Smack your butt on the ground, then hop up and do whatever you please," though without enforcement, that's how a pup typically responds when made to sit, especially when among peers. While it's true that no pup should be pressured, force can scare him at a time when the young one is highly vulnerable. It's equally true that no dog should ever be taught that a command allows a choice, especially during the impression-able phase of puppyhood.

Puppy-class advocates contend that a correction is added to the program when the pooch is old enough to handle it. That's a mixed signal. To initially demonstrate that a command is open to a vote and then to change the rule later is a sure way to instill confusion and distrust in any animal.

A second problem with puppy classes has to do with trainer attitude. A professed puppy-class aim is to demonstrate that obedience is a fun and pleasant activity. That's a valid sentiment, but I've know its expression to have a boomerang effect. Some novice trainers come away with the erroneous impression that when serious teaching is commenced months later, the "fun and pleasant activity" element is no longer appropriate because the animal is no longer a puppy. Of course, a positive attitude should be constant: It should operate in any training program, regardless of a dog's age.

Feeding

From a canine perspective, the giving of food is a meaningful act: It's what Mom used to do. Assuming you're using a dry kibble (which I recommend, as the nutritional value is consistent and dependable), pour the pellets over your hand and into the bowl, to associate your scent with the food. Rather than calling pooch to a food bowl already placed on the ground, bring him to the eating area and then present the dish so that there's no doubt as to its origin. Of course, don't remove a bowl while the animal is in mid-bite, but allow only ten minutes or so for consuming a meal. Dogs are naturally fast eaters: In the wild, one eats as quickly as possible, lest others covet the meal or circumstances cause its abandonment.

Avoid *on-demand feeding*, whereby food is available at all times. That can result in boredom, finicky eating habits and obesity. Of equal importance, it eliminates from a canine's emotional menu the opportunity for intimate daily contacts between dog and leader, which has as much to do with positive bonding as with proper nutrition. Scheduled meals also afford the advantage of signaling that an animal has gone off feed, which can be the first hint of numerous physical and psychological disorders.

Snacks and Such

As far as when tidbits are appropriate—and when they are not—consider this example: When calling pooch into the house, present a biscuit once he arrives indoors. Rather than make this a constant practice, reward about three times out of four. Make do with petting when a snack isn't given. That way, curiosity as to whether there will be a treat can operate and draw him to you.

However, don't use food to bribe. That is, don't stand by the door and wave the tidbit while calling the animal. That implies the biscuit will be given whether puppy comes just then or not. Offering your dog the choice to obey or ignore your wishes isn't a good idea at any age: Pooch could decide he'd rather persist at whatever he's doing than stop for a snack just then. Get the animal inside, then present the morsel.

Housing and Housebreaking

Though written from the standpoint of puppy rearing, elements of the following, such as nest training, can be applied to older dogs as well. Practices pertaining specifically to pups, such as carrying the animal to a designated outside area, are obvious.

A new puppy should sleep at bedside in a properly sized, individual airline-type crate. This practice can eliminate much grief from housebreaking because a sound animal won't consistently foul the sleeping area, assuming he's given ample opportunity to seek relief at suitable locations.

Afford puppy a final evening walk at bedtime, then take him straightaway to the crate. When first placing the pup in the enclosure, do so gently while softly repeating, "Nest," several times. The word best expresses the idea to communicate to the little one. A weekend is often an opportune time to acquaint puppy with the nest, as some sleep may be lost the first night. To lessen undue worry and whining, place in the crate ahead of time such puppy treasures as a soft towel, maybe a ticking clock (which can be reminiscent of Mom's heartbeat), possibly a safe chew or perhaps an undergarment you wore that day (probably for the last time). Don't let a dog, young or old, shred a cloth article—ingestion of such material can be fatal.

A pup finding himself alone in this new situation may whine and fuss some, but after a time he'll usually settle. If the young one becomes unreasonably vocal and if you're certain he's not telling you he *must* get outside, soft words and finger contact through the crate door can do wonders.

Don't move the nest about the house unless absolutely necessary. Part of its function is to create a sense of order and stability in and for a puppy. Periodic crate relocation can defeat that purpose. Similarly, other pets or children shouldn't be permitted to enter or play with the crate. The enclosure is something the young canine needs to think of as his, and his nose will tell him if there have been visitors.

The very first thing in the morning, take puppy outdoors, repeating the cue "Yard" as you transport him. If the nest is some distance from the door, prevent undesirable stops along the way by carrying him. Once he's back inside, keep your attention on him. Should you be occupied with an activity for a time, put puppy in the nest before proceeding.

Bear in mind that puppies initially possess very little control. An active pup involved in play and such would rather continue with what he's doing than stop to expel toxins. Thus, nature has so constructed him that until he gains some maturity, he's unable to hold back the dam for more than a few seconds after his little brain issues the word. Once you see "that look" in his eyes, you've very little time to get him outside.

The first time puppy does goof in the house—and most do at least once—point his nose close to (but not into) the site of the transgression and repeat the word "No" in a firm, drawn-out manner. Don't speak harshly—that could frighten him. More than one overly vocal owner has taught through displays of righteous temper that the animal's natural urges were wrong. "Not here" is the message to communicate, not shame.

After drawing attention to the problem area, tote the puppy outside, encouragingly saying the word "Yard" as you proceed. Gathering up the accident and placing it at the location you want frequented can be helpful. Puppy will soon get the idea.

As pup performs outside, praise (but softly, so as not to distract), saying, "Good piddle, good dump," or whatever phraseology you prefer. Later, during lengthy drives, cueing your pet at a rest stop to "Go piddle" can trigger the desired response.

During puppy's waking hours, regardless of whether he sends signals, make sure to take him outside every few hours. Also, walk him after naps, meals and prolonged drinking. Those are times when pups often feel the need.

Unless you've no choice, avoid using newspapers for relief sites. "Paper training" is just that—it can teach a dog to respond to the feel of paper underfoot. More importantly, the animal is being taught to use the

The author as Alpha, exercising a litter of Doberman Pinscher puppies.

house as a bathroom. Sure, he's standing on yesterday's *Daily Bugle*, but that doesn't change the fact that elimination is occurring in your living space.

Exercise and Socialization

Proper exercise is as important to canine well-being as is proper nutrition. Without both, healthy physiological or psychological development can't occur. Your pet needs plenty of play area and lots of playtime with you.

Socialization entails taking pooch with you wherever and whenever circumstances permit. This is especially true for pups. During life's first months, the number and quality of situations, people and events a pup experiences will affect him for all time. Always keeping him on leash, take your companion to public parks, school areas or just for a drive. If you intend for your pet to be a member of your pack (family), treat him like one.

When taking a dog (young or mature) for outings, *never* leave him unattended in a vehicle, not even for just a few minutes. The result can be chewed seats, a stolen pet or heatstroke. That last is often fatal and can occur very quickly on a bright day with outside temperatures no warmer than 70 degrees.

Teething

Pups begin cutting permanent teeth around sixteen weeks. Ease this uncomfortable time by providing safe chewing items. Gently massaging the young one's gums not only alleviates discomfort; it strengthens the bond forming between you.

Protection

Prudence dictates taking precautions for your dog's safety. One is an area securely fenced to a minimum height of five feet. That may seem excessive if yours is a small animal, but bear in mind that while a fence is intended to contain, it's also designed to keep intruders out. There are those who take things not belonging to them, your pet included. The size of the area need not be huge: The idea is to create sufficient room to pace.

Two other safeguards are a watchful eye and scant patience with anyone who teases. Dogs possessing even minimum intelligence and spirit seldom tolerate such abuse for long, and they shouldn't have to.

Discourage anyone who feels compelled to affect an agitating posture in the presence of a large dog. Similarly, waste no patience on the clown who habitually ridicules smaller canines. Such a person's frail ego may need the stimulation, but pooch's spirit is your first concern.

Don't tie a dog. The practice can easily induce paranoia (as well as aggressiveness), since the animal's primary defense—flight—has been taken from him. Also, tying can create distrust toward yourself, as it's you who've done the taking.

I never allow my dogs off leash in a public area, regardless of the animal's age or training depth. I don't ever want to find myself in a courtroom trying to phrase a disarming reply to the learned judge's query "Has the dog been trained to bite?" That a child was nipped while trying to stick the animal in the eye may prove a shallow defense. Without exception, if your dog is even bite trained, keep him on leash whenever you are both out in public; otherwise, you open a door to disaster.

Reflection

Dogs naturally run in packs, following the strongest personalities therein as leaders thereof. Your pup takes you for the lead dog. So you behave, hear? Don't mess up your image.

L. M. Boyd

4

Instincts and Drives

THOUGH BOOKS have been written on this chapter's subjects, my intent is to touch on just the high points; to present the essentials of instinctual and drive behavior without getting bogged down in endless theories and scientific minutiae.

Capsulized

Instincts and drives are at once closely related yet separate types of innate motivating forces. Differentiating between them can spark heated debate in a psychology class. For our purposes, drives are behaviors that satisfy instinctual demands.

In terms of cause and effect, instincts are *general* inborn urges to act toward satiation of basic needs (hunger, shelter, safety etc.). Drives are *specific* behaviors a dog effectuates in attempts to satisfy these needs. A canine doesn't think about these responses—he simply does them. As a very knowledgeable trainer once generalized, "Drive is what makes the dog chase the rabbit."

While it's hardly the purpose of *Dog Logic* to reduce the essence of *Canis familiaris* to little more than a tidy array of physiological and psychological nuts and bolts, canine actions are undeniably a product of inborn behaviors modified by learning. Instincts and drives are rooted in genetics—each dog is born with them to varying degrees. Learned behavior results from experience gained during applications of genetically motivated behaviors or of other learned behaviors.

For instance, dogs have an instinct to survive. They satisfy this instinct through self-preservation drives, some of which are the drive to hunt, tracking drive, prey drive, retrieve drive, self-defense drive and the drive to flee.

A Behavior by Any Other Name . . .

Keep in mind that genetic motivators of behavior—whether they're called instincts, drives, needs, internal stimuli or by some other term—achieve identical results. For instance, I view canine knowledge about *tracking* (following a scent trail) as a drive. Others assert that tracking is instinctual behavior. To pigeonhole tracking as instinctive- or drive-sponsored behavior can be debated interminably. The salient point is that dogs are born with the capability to track; it's not a learned behavior. When one says he's teaching a canine to track, in truth the animal is being taught to perform on cue. Effective practice improves proficiency, but the dog already knew how to track. He was born with the knowledge.

Real World

For an example of the interaction between instincts, drives and learned behaviors, consider how a young, inexperienced dog might deal with hunger.

First, the body communicates the need for energy to the brain through biochemical means. The brain interprets these signals and causes the dog to feel the discomfort of being hungry. This sensation is a biological response that triggers another sequence of physiological and psychological events that lead the animal to resolve the problem through drive behavior.

The dog begins to *hunt* for *prey* and is soon *tracking* a scent trail he's discovered. Unfortunately, the critter he's tracking in our scenario is a porcupine. Assuming the dog finds and attempts to overcome the beast, he soon learns that this particular type of creature is more than he can handle. The *drive to flee* rushes to the forefront as the need to satisfy hunger—a transient condition—is suddenly overridden by the longer-term *instinct to survive*, to be able to hunt for prey another day.

The pup in our example doesn't give up trying to satisfy hunger, however. He cannot. Survival instinct is too strong for that. Later, he perhaps encounters a small fowl or rodent and is successful in transforming the animal into a canine repast *du jour*. He learns from these experiences that while four-footed pincushions are best left alone, feathered walkers and/or small furry creatures can be used in relative safety to satisfy hunger.

All this constitutes instinctual demands being satisfied by drive behaviors modified by learning. In a nutshell, that's the basis of canine motivation. For us, it's the pathway toward an understanding and appreciation of various approaches to canine obedience training.

INSTINCTS

To avoid needless complications, the only instincts we as trainers need to acknowledge are the instinct to survive (the primary force underlying all others), the pack instinct and the instinct for freedom. The study of other inborn canine tendencies, such as the motivation to circle prior to lying down, is more akin to intellectual gymnastics than essential information.

Survival Instinct: The primary message of this self-evident genetic knowledge is "I must endure!" It's the reason an injured canine may strike out blindly toward the hand of his owner, who is only trying to help. Though it may seem a paradox, the power of the survival instinct is such that a dog can be made to learn to accept extreme environmental pressure (abuse) as a condition of survival (see *Learned-helplessness syndrome* in the Glossary). Many obedience programs are wrongly keyed on stimulating this instinct.

Pack Instinct: Stated simply, this inner force leads dogs toward a familylike life-style as compared to a hermitlike existence. Appealing to this instinct provides the basis for effective, reasonable training.

Freedom Instinct: Dogs, although social animals that prefer companionship over perpetual solitude, are by nature neither clingers nor slaves. Each is his own animal. Lack of awareness and appreciation of this instinct has led many trainers to confuse its behavioral manifestations with rebellion. Understanding this inborn motivator's influence and effect on canine behavior is essential for shaping attitude toward obedience. Rather than attempting to thwart this instinct, thereby knocking down spirit, put the communicative accent on appealing to the pack instinct. Show the dog that submission to human leadership is a by-product of the person's desire for pack contact; that it represents human attraction to the canine's essence, not a diminution of the dog's self.

DRIVES

Following is a list of canine drives. Some trainers combine certain of them under single, more comprehensive headings, and others further subclassify and thereby expand the list. While most agree that drives can be grouped under one of three headings—self-preservation, species-preservation or self- and species-preservation—some might argue that a given drive belongs in column "B" rather than in column "C." This is one of the reasons why I told you in the preface that canine training books are "a work of opinion and conjecture."

Self-Preservation Drives

Drives that support self-preservation:

Air scenting: The motivation to discern airborne scents and investigate them.

Flight: The drive to rapidly depart from the area of an overpowering threat, whether real or imagined.

Hunting: The desire to search for and locate prey.

Play: This drive is growth-oriented in that it leads a dog to explore and test his abilities to contend with others.

Prey: This underlies the motivation to attack and kill prey. Like the hunting drive, the prey drive is rooted in the need to satisfy hunger.

Retrieving: Interrelated with hunting and prey drives, this motivator leads a dog to move captured prey from one location to another.

Self-defense: This is willingness to fight in one's own defense. Like the flight drive, it's a fear response. When taken to extremes, self-defense against imagined threats is what drives the fear biter.

Tracking: Similar to the drive to air scent, the tracking drive leads a dog to investigate and follow ground-scent disturbances.

Drives to Preserve the Species

Drives that relate to preserving the species:

Dominance: This is the motivator to lead the pack. When present to extremes, we find the bold, strong-willed and often-hard-to-train canine at one end of the continuum and the super submissive dog at the other. The former frequently contests attempts at control, while the latter spends a good deal of time effecting flat-on-his-back submission.

Guard: This is the tendency to inform the pack that intruders are entering the area, the territory.

Sex: This drive is the basis for canine reproductive activities.

Maternal: This drive is what leads a dam to support her pups through nursing, cleaning and general care.

Protection: Closely linked to the drive to guard (some trainers claim the two are inseparable), this quality leads a canine to protect members of his or her pack.

Self-Preservation/Species Preservation Drives

Drives to preserve each individual and to preserve the species:

Cooperation: This is the motivator to get along with members of the pack in general and with the pack leader specifically.

Fighting: Canines possessing a good deal of this drive often enjoy a good scrap. It's an essential trait for a pack leader.

Homing: The presence of this drive leads a dog back to the den. It comprises much of the basis for teaching pooch to come when called.

Visual

For clarity, the instincts and drives referred to in this chapter are presented below in diagram form:

INSTINCTS AND DRIVES

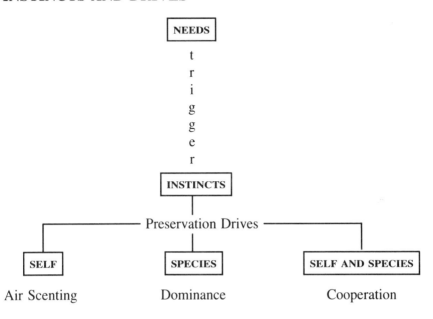

Flight   Guard   Fighting

Hunting Maternal Homing

Play   Protection

Prey   Sex

Retrieving

Self-Defense

Tracking

Relevance

Many drives contribute to creating a training foundation. While reference is made in later chapters to the relevancy of certain drives to specific lessons, to correlate each and every obedience exercise with this or that instinct or drive would make this chapter one of the book's longer ones and would only be of minor technical interest. Suffice it to say that were the pack and the freedom instincts and the drives for cooperation, hunting, play, prey, retrieving and homing not present in dogs, the subject of canine training would be mostly theoretical.

Reflection

The dog always lives in the here and now and is unable to understand the reasons for his own actions.

Johannes Grewe,
The Police Service Dog

5

Training Guidelines

THIS CHAPTER contains general guidance for connecting with man's best buddy. Additional principles and specific techniques accompany corresponding lessons presented in subsequent chapters.

Obedience Training Defined

Obedience training is a process through which a person takes control of and enhances mutual bonding with his or her dog by developing a basis for and means of significant communication. It regulates canine behavior by making the animal responsible for it. The person who applies obedience training says, in effect, to a dog, "You and I are together. Because I am dominant, I will lead and direct."

Now, you walk up to most humans and drop that line on them and you're liable to find yourself in a running fistfight. But this is a dog's training under discussion, not a person's. As suggested in chapter 1, when properly communicated, a sound canine recognizes the sentiment for what it is, and the response is positive. That's a pack attribute (and a main endearment). Conversely, offensive communication, from spurious playacting to overbearing inflexibility, may produce obedience of a sort, but its long-term influence dulls instinctual attraction to the leader.

Obedience Training's Objective

Obedience training teaches several forms of work: Sit, Lie Down, Stay, Come, Heel and so forth. In so doing, it satisfies a dog's need for pack responsibility and identity. While the exercises have intrinsic value by providing control, their overall purpose is to make a dog responsive to the handler. Less conspicuous obedience goals, then, are tuning your pet's ear to the sound of your voice, telling the animal that you desire contact, that you have things to teach, that you two are a team.

Some Things Never Change

Consider Max Von Stephanitz's 1925 observation:

> Whoever can find the answer to the question, "How shall I say this to my dog?", has won the game and can develop from his animal whatever he likes.*

Those timeless words bespeak the essence of training, the "why" of it. Handlers sometimes blow right past the truism that there are reasons why training techniques do or don't work. A procedure is effective not because someone says it is: It's effective when and because a dog "says" it is. A pooch "says" that training is effective when the method produces a confident, reliable, happy worker. It's all very well to memorize a prominent trainer's system, but if one doesn't understand how and why "these things" work (or why they don't), the individual is training in the dark.

Semantics

Training occurs through three phases: First is *teaching*, the imparting of new material, new lessons. Second is *integration*, bringing separate exercises together into a coherent whole. The third phase, *conditioning*, or acclimating, is practicing under increasing distractions and in unfamiliar settings those routines a dog has learned. All these elements taken together comprise *training*.

Ultimately, training leads to *performance*, which is applying conditioned learning to practical situations. That final phase is aptly termed *working*, but in the lexicon of many trainers (myself included), *working*

---

*Max von Stephanitz, *The German Shepherd Dog in Word and Picture* (Arvada, Colo.: Hoflin Publishing, 1982), p. 564.

(as in "working a dog") is also synonymous with any of the three elements of training.

Now for the "rules."

TRAINING SESSIONS

When and When Not

The time for effective training is when you have ample time and aren't distracted by other concerns. It is *not* when either of you is tired or ill or when you are pressed for time, irritated or are otherwise preoccupied. The risk is transmitting negative feelings your dog could interpret as indicating some undefined displeasure with him. That can produce baseless anxiety in a relationship that should be worry-free.

Thank You for Not Smoking

Smokers: Shelve the habit during training and play periods. Tobacco scent can overpower a canine's acute nose. Your friend will avoid the harsh smell on your breath, hands and clothing. In so doing he's learning to avoid *you*. Obviously, teaching pooch to evade or feel discomfort in your presence is incompatible with bonding. Besides, the activity is distractive, causing momentary lapses of concentration. You have enough to keep your mind occupied without external interferences.

No Shades, Either

Leave dark glasses in the house. Contact is a vital training concept, and eye contact tops the list. A dog that can't see your eyes will eventually quit trying to. He learns not to look your way, which is exactly the wrong attitude to foster.

Only You for Now

For the first few weeks, it's preferable that pooch have but one trainer: you. A dog can experience enough learning difficulties without the added confusion of one teacher's voice being markedly different from another's. "Sit!" for example, spoken in a deep voice, can sound different from "Sit!" spoken in a high voice. Similarly, men often take a longer and sometimes quicker stride than women. By rotating trainers prematurely, a canine can run into problems learning heeling.

As Time Goes By

Within a few weeks, you may begin to transfer training to a second handler, such as your spouse. However, a child who is physically or psychologically unable to back up his or her commands should not work a dog. A canine that perceives incapability can learn to ignore the giver's commands and may come to resent his or her attentions.

Before a Training Period

Don't exercise or work your pet sooner than an hour after feeding. Doing so can not only invite cramping; it can lessen performance: A hungry dog works better. Also, provide ample opportunity to seek relief before work or play.

Are you familiar with a concept known as the six P's? It's been stated in differing forms, some more colorful than others, but essentially it declares: *Prior Planning Prevents Pitifully Poor Performance*. Its training application is mapping out each practice, anticipating your dog's likely reactions to given circumstances and determining how you'll respond. As with most forms of endeavor, effective training results from being conducted in neither random nor haphazard manner.

No Initial Distractions

Teach in a distraction-free, securely fenced area. The notion that a dog is best taught in or near stressful surroundings is false. Distraction work (conditioning) should be delayed until the integration phase (which follows the teaching phase) has been under way for several weeks.

Consistent Training Location

Confine the first weeks of training to a single location. Your dog will come to see that the area is special: It's not only a place for learning but for correct deportment as well. The environment itself acts as an attitude reinforcer. Once pooch is responding properly to several commands, periodically move practice sessions to distractive, real-world locations.

Your Pack

Family members may attend practices but *not initial teaching sessions*. The last thing that either of you needs during instruction periods is the distractive, pressuring influence of family members. When attending practices, they should not use the animal's name or attempt to establish eye contact with him. Otherwise, confusion can arise, and your dog can learn to distrust other members of the family—his pack.

It's Called Commitment

Be consistent in your training schedule. That's not to say, "Train daily at 5:17 P.M." but to train at least five days weekly. Pooch doesn't need a periodic day off. You may, but a dog doesn't. Properly staged, he'll look forward to the sessions.

How Long?

Work your pet in fifteen- to twenty-minute periods. Twice a day is optimum, with several hours between sessions. As you train for twenty minutes a day, play with pooch for twenty minutes a day (but not during the same twenty minutes).

Class Versus Recess

For now, keep playtime separate from work periods. Your dog should wear the training collar during both activities (thereby building a pleasant association toward the object via the fun of the play sessions), but no commands should be given during play. Doing so prematurely can stifle enthusiasm.

End High

End each training period on a positive note, with your dog performing an exercise successfully. Never quit in failure. To do so can lead your pet to carry a negative attitude into the next practice and inhibit him toward work. If pooch is having "one of those days," command a simple exercise he knows well (like Sit) and close the session with a flourish of praise to finish with a success. Don't give commands while leaving the training area: Should the dog err and be disciplined, the end-high concept is defeated.

So as Not to Hinder Learning

Right after training, avoid involving your friend in another activity (including feeding, but do allow access to water) so as not to risk distracting him after the fact. Rather than possibly overriding recent learning, encourage the passage of some quiet, contemplative time, free of new mental input that might interfere with absorption of the previous few minutes' lessons.

RULES OF TECHNIQUE

Go to the Dog's Level

I've mentioned this concept before, but it's of such significance that it bears repeating. In any dealings with a canine you must operate at the animal's level of understanding; it's a certainty he can't be brought to yours. No, I'm not suggesting you learn to bay at the moon or develop a taste for dog biscuits. I'm saying that communication must occur in a manner a dog can comprehend. Obviously, it's of scant purpose to dictate, "See here, dog: When I command, you comply," yet I've known otherwise rational people who expected results from essentially that approach.

Remember, the dog is the animal that turns around several times before lying down, to flatten grass and look for snakes—even when he's standing on your rug! He lives in a world far apart from ours, one he cannot elect to abandon.

Communicating at a dog's plane of reality often entails incorporating subtle body language into the teaching program. It's a canine's nature to react to such communication. For instance, leaning slightly away from a nervous or standoffish dog often attracts more focus than does a looming mother-hen posture. The former invites contact; the latter can stifle.

Teach Close

Lessons are best taught by keeping pooch in close proximity to you. That may seem obvious, but some training systems start with distance work, usually in the form of Stays followed by Recalls. ("Come to me.") It's better to begin by teaching certain exercises (such as Sit, Lie Down and Stay) close to you, gradually increasing distance only after learning has occurred. To initially teach at a distance is not only impractical; it also hampers the bonding process, for it teaches that distance is an element of the relationship.

"A," Then "B," Then "C" . . .

Present one lesson at a time. For example, when teaching Sit, don't initially be concerned with where the dog sits. Some folks teach the command simultaneous with teaching the Heel position (facing forward at the handler's left side), but that's covering two elements at once. Such a technique is not only unwise; it's unfair (as you'll see in chapter 8, "First Week").

One must acknowledge canine cognitive limitations. Animals at the intelligence level of *Canis familiaris* best learn only one thing, or a short chain of things, during a single session. This is especially true when initiating schooling. That's when it's easiest to confuse an otherwise willing dog by expecting mastery of too many elements at once. Complex work must be taught a step at a time. Strongest foundations are created by teaching concepts singly, thereby maximizing learning potential.

"A," Then "B," Then "C" Revisited

When conducting lessons already taught, practice them separately. For example, after teaching pooch about heeling and to lie down, do a few minutes of heeling, *then* a few minutes of lying down.

Two motives underlie this guideline. First, should a dog have difficulty with an exercise, his negative feelings toward the problem can spill into the other activity and inhibit progress that might otherwise be made. Second, until a canine internalizes a lesson, he can better focus on it if his concentration isn't distracted by another requirement.

"How will I know when to move on to integrated practice?"

Any two exercises can usually be practiced together after four to seven days of teaching the more recent element. Again, the "If in doubt, don't!" principle applies, as a main purpose of delaying the integration phase is to avoid stress.

Teaching Versus Polishing

One cannot reasonably expect instant perfection. When teaching a dog to lie down on command, for example, don't lose any sleep if pooch initially lies on his side or back rather than in an alert, straight position. In nearly all cases, a canine matures past any tendencies to lie on his side or back faster than the precise position can be taught. As suggested earlier, it causes less stress for both dog and trainer to teach approximates, polishing the work over time. In the long-term view of producing a happy, reliable worker, better a dog learn from success than failure. Accept your pet's best attempts for what they are: his present best. He'll do better with time and encouragement. Fine-tune as you go along.

Curveball Teaching

Another useful principle is *obfuscation*, which is a nine-dollar word that alludes to teaching one pattern of behavior to circumvent resistance born of difficulty with another. For instance, the dog that steadfastly refuses to lie down can often be taught to do so on a large scrap of carpet, provided he's made to lie down there and nowhere else. Not only does the carpet remnant act as both a stimulus and a reinforcer; canine curiosity operates in such a situation. It draws the animal's attention away from resistance and redirects it to an object related to the desired behavior. Gradually reduce the rug's size until it ceases to exist.

Same Chorus, Second Verse

A variation on the preceding idea is to teach a resistant dog more than is actually expected. Speaking again about lying down, one can teach that the command directs pooch to lie down *and* to place head on paws. Then the trainer can settle for the animal merely lying down, which was the objective all along.

No, this isn't teaching two lessons at once. "Sit" and "Where to sit" are distinct concepts. "Lie down" and "like this" aren't. The former deals with "what" and "where," the latter with "what" and "how."

Dealing with Resistance, Part III

A more head-on method for overcoming obstinacy is to work only on the resisted exercise until compliance results. Should Sit be the bone of contention, focus solely on that element during training periods. Do no heeling, no lying down, no stays and so on. Concentrate on Sit until the animal accedes.

Focus

During training sessions keep your total and unwavering attention on pooch: It's the easiest way to capture his. As a dog should rivet attention on the handler, said handler does well to teach by example— that is, by maintaining his or her own concentration on the student. If a

An example of noncontact.

trainer is otherwise distracted, training is not truly occurring. The person isn't totally present at the situation because the mind is elsewhere. Your aspect must say that there is you and your dog—nothing else matters. Remember the timeworn adage: Whatever attitude you send down the leash comes back to you.

That May Seem Evident, but . . .

True, the foregoing counsel belabors the obvious, but trainers often pay their charges scant attention. Such indifference is absurd and may be unintentional, but watch beginning trainers (and, sometimes, experienced ones), especially during heeling. A handler commands, "Heel," and directs his attention several feet ahead as he begins walking. A cat could be substituted at the leash's end and the person would be unaware of the switch until he stopped moving (or effected a collar correction).

Understand, I'm not suggesting that it's either necessary or desirable for you to go through life staring at your pet. In time you'll be so in tune with him that the need for concentrated visual contact will lessen. The degree of attention required to stay in touch decreases as skills, proficiency and contact grow.

Time Out

Bear in mind that any animal can have an off day. If my dog has been progressing satisfactorily but one day seems out of sorts, I end the session with the intent of having another go at it on the morrow. For all I know, the animal has a splitting headache. If the following day brings no improvement, we go to the vet or the mat, depending on which course seems apropos.

Excessive Repetition

Expect your pet to be getting the idea by the third or fourth demonstration of any new lesson. Slow learners exist, but dogs generally catch on quickly. The concept that pooch must be shown a given thing umpteen times belies canine nature. Such technique is understandably boring to you both. Worse, it can say that pooch'll never have to perform the work himself; that you'll always help him through it. Recall that in his natural setting a dog might have but a single learning opportunity, lest he become another's dinner. Thus, nature has programmed him to assimilate knowledge quickly.

Get It Right

When a dog misperforms work already learned, repeat the botched lesson quickly four to six times consecutively without appreciable error. This technique clarifies responsibility, promotes mental extinction of the incorrect response and enables successful completion of the exercise.

Don't Leapfrog

Don't give a novice animal commands you can't immediately back up physically. If you've taught pooch to Sit on command near you, for example, don't jump to commanding Sit at great distances. Without employing the technique of gradually increasing distance, your pet can learn to ignore not only specific commands but the sound of your voice as well.

Impossible Situations

As no being operates with perfection, any dog eventually misperforms any task if made to repeat it ad infinitum. Ergo, refrain from pursuing any exercise for such a lengthy time that what you're actually doing is guaranteeing pooch a correction (application of force). That's cruelty, pure and simple. Besides, if an animal does as well as he's then able, it's illogical to repeat the work right away: No likelihood of improvement currently exists.

Back Off

Should pooch experience uncharacteristic difficulty with an exercise, allow time for confusion to fade by dropping the lesson for a few days or weeks. Then reteach it via a different method and a dissimilar-sounding command, presenting it as new material. The technique is far easier than attempting to fight through accumulated resistance to an old command. Repeated use of a term that a dog associates with negative feelings only reinforces his bias. When replacing a command, *do not* link it in any way with the former cue.

INTEGRATION AND CONDITIONING

Integration

This phase is characterized by practicing exercises in sequence. It's akin to the method by which athletes and teams learn routines and plays.

Work that Animal Fast

Once training has progressed to the integration phase, work pooch quickly. I don't just mean that you should walk hurriedly during heeling, for instance, but that you should go from exercise to exercise with dispatch. As one routine ends, praise and begin another. This stimulating style of practice challenges a dog, thereby heightening his enjoyment of the proceedings. It also has the effect of capturing and maintaining attention—he hasn't time for anything but you. Lastly, instilling this working attitude helps to take an animal past any residual contention: There's simply no time for him to display any objections he might harbor.

Conditioning

Conditioning is practicing integrated material in altered or unfamiliar, increasingly distractive settings. Running through familiar exercises while children play near the training area is a good initial distraction. A continuation would be training near a busy Little League park.

Worthwhile disturbances are animals, people, traffic settings, gunfire and bitches in season. Don't use the removal of your pet's food dish, full or empty as a distraction. That's an unfair tactic that can lead to pointless anxiety. Using a menacing or abnormally behaving person as a distraction in training is also ill-advised. It's unwise to put a canine in a threatening situation with the intent of thwarting his natural drive to protect.

Initially using play objects as training distractions can lessen drive or attraction for the article. In extreme cases, a dog could even come to distrust or fear the object. Later, after your pet has had much practice with formal obedience, the toy can and should be used for distraction conditioning (requiring him to heel past the play toy, for example, to say that your wishes transcend his). However, during initial training, keep toys removed from working sessions.

Hither and Yon

Once the conditioning phase has been initiated, vary practice times and locations, working indoors as well as out and in all reasonable weather. It's neither necessary nor wise to train in subzero temperatures or at high noon during a heat wave. Convincing pooch that obedience is enjoyable, a program objective can be difficult when he's either freezing or tripping over his tongue. It is appropriate, though, to demonstrate that commands don't lose validity in a light rain or because it's two o'clock in the morning.

COMMANDS

Commands Defined

Commands cue canine behavior. A command doesn't just state "You should do this thing," but, "You *will* do this thing—now!"

Commands are often perceived as being synonymous with orders, or dictates. Trainers think of them as cues. Had canines a thesaurus, they'd likely choose the synonym "warning," not in the sense of a threat but as a portent, or sign. Audible cues between pack members in the wild often are warnings.

"This Word Means . . . and You Will Do It"

It's one thing to teach a dog what a particular command signifies; it's another matter to say that commands aren't open to a vote. A person can spend numerous training sessions showing what "Sit!" (for example) means in terms of a body position, but until the trainer also says to the dog that Sit (or any other command) means "You must!" one cannot fairly hold the animal accountable. Be clear with your pet about this tenet of coexistence. Any directives to your pet must always include the notion "Dog, when I command, you comply, and there's an end of it."

Cues Within Cues

Obedience commands are of one syllable, while guard commands are of two syllables. The rationale behind this practice is to build a safety valve into protection work: It takes two "barks" to send a dog, one to stop him. It also makes for a quicker obedience worker.

Uno!

Here's the briefest lesson: In nearly all situations (I'll mention exceptions as we go along), give each command only once; not twice, thrice or sixteen times—once! To repeat a command is to absolve the dog from accountability. Besides, if the animal doesn't respond correctly the first time, he either couldn't hear you, is confused or just expressed his opinion about obeying.

He Knows Who You're Talking To

Don't use your companion's name in conjunction with commands. The sound of the (pack) leader's voice provides all the keys a dog needs. The use of your pet's name is for when you and he are talking—visiting—not for when you're working.

Besides . . .

Canine mental processes are remarkably fast, and to precede each command with the name is to allow attention to wander. A dog can learn he has sufficient time to let his mind drift, returning his focus to the situation during the interval between the name and the command. If pooch is shown from day one that a single, one-syllable command is all the cue he'll receive, his attention will remain where it belongs: on you.

Overkill

A related consideration is that if commands are always preceded with the dog's name, the animal hears it so much that attraction to it is desensitized. Overuse can teach him to ignore its sound.

Think about it. If a handler precedes each command with the dog's name during a twenty-five-command workout, the animal hears the name twenty-five times. Multiply that by five or six sessions per week and that's too much. It can easily burn out a dog toward the sound of his name. While not intending to anthropomorphize, if you were to hear your name after every other word during a conversation, you'd likely become bored (or self-conscious) with its sound.

Some argue that using a dog's name when working is a cue similar to "Attention!" All that tells me is that the dog's concentration is being lost between exercises.

Communication.

Only When You Mean It

Command only when you intend to. For instance, telling your pal when leaving the house, "Now, you *stay here*," diminishes in his mind the command to Stay as well as the command to come to you ("Here"). Why? Because while you're away, pooch won't Stay (remain in one place), and he's thereby taught that Stay carries overtones of Remain in one place, unless you think you can get away with moving. "Here" likewise becomes a vehicle of confusion since your dog obviously can't come to you when you aren't present.

Go for It

Give one clear, decisive command and proceed, with no hesitation in your next move. A cue that isn't coupled with action results in lost rhythm and fragmented attention. As noted earlier, dogs avoid uncertainty and indecision whenever possible. Exhibiting such mannerisms can teach a dog to associate anxiety with obedience generally and the trainer specifically.

Talk Like a Friend

Communicate in your normal speaking voice, lest you inhibit, threaten or beg rather than command. Only as you begin to work at increasing distances or in crowded traffic situations does it become necessary to raise the sound level. When your friend is inches from you, command accordingly, using your normal voice.

Has Anyone Ever Yelled in Your Ear?

Some trainers improperly overemphasize command volume. They give commands to their animals from a distance of two feet as if they were two blocks away. It's a mind-set similar to that which holds that when attempting to communicate with someone who is not fluent in one's own language, raising one's voice and speaking ultra slowly, with exaggerated enunciation, will get the message across.

Canine hearing is far more acute than ours, and a normal voice captures and holds attention far longer than a loud one. Overmodulated tones desensitize receptiveness, leading a dog to tune out the handler. Emotionally overpowering a softly temperamented canine is a risk of excessive decibels, as is igniting the fuse of an overly dominant animal. The former will try to mentally hide from the sound, and the latter can perceive booming volume as threatening.

All Coins Have Two Sides

Folks who insist on baby talk verbally inhibit bonding more than the bellowers. It's plastic. It's not you. Once, while listening to an owner hit notes registering above high C in praising her pooch, I overheard a revered trainer from Germany mutter, "That makes the dog silly."

He's right. A canine thus belittled can instantly transform into something of an emotional Froot Loop. To display attitudes not a normal part of your personality is deception, which a dog quickly discerns as contrived behavior. One can include enthusiasm in his or her voice without becoming extreme or false. Like uncertainty, insincerity makes a canine ill at ease. As an acquaintance once observed, "Kids and dogs—they know."

Look at it this way. Do you remember the aged relative who patted you on the head and spoke to you as though you were still four years old—even though you'd voted in two presidential elections? Your dog doesn't appreciate *his best friend* putting on a front for him, either. He sees it as unreal, and unreal attributes make a dog nervous. It's as though he knows that the unreal can't exist in nature, and the contradiction is too much for him.

Neither approach, whether overly loud or infantile, communicates sincerity to one as keenly perceptive as a canine. The usual result is to impart a sense of uncertainty, which is the last thing needed in an intimate relationship. Uncertainty and hesitation can defeat an otherwise sound working prospect.

Because a dog can't verbalize, he pays more attention to your tones than to your words. Evolution has enhanced his capacity to detect unvoiced emotion. In a very real sense, your dog hears your inner voice.

Between the Lines

The messages your commands radiate should include "Come with me. Watch me. I'm glad you're with me." You can accomplish this more effectively using unspoken communication and subtle animation than through loquaciousness and histrionics.

"What if He Didn't Hear Me?"

This is an exception to the rule of giving a command only once. If you're working at a great distance in a very noisy environment and you're convinced pooch was unable to hear, of course you should repeat the command. The animal certainly shouldn't be disciplined for failure to comply; he couldn't have known that there was anything to be complied with. Nor should one pressure a dog that seems confused or inhibited by the situation in which he's found himself. He's just saying that conditioning is being brought along too fast. On the other hand, if your friend is right next to you in a calm setting and should he fail to respond to a command due to inattention, don't repeat the order—correct him.

DRIVE AND COMPULSION/PRAISE AND CORRECTION

Drive and Compulsion

Training is rooted in drive and compulsion. Either mode can reinforce the other, as you'll see.

Drive training is teaching and reinforcing by appealing to appropriate drives mentioned in chapter 4, "Instincts and Drives." Drive work can also be thought of as animation, or positive motivation, and is symbolically akin to *praise*. It teaches by affording a canine something he wants, often in areas where the animal cannot be made to do a given thing. For example, a dog can be physically forced to sit, but he can't be forced to like it. That's where drive training comes in.

Compulsion can be likened to force, or negative motivation. Often spoken of as *correction*, it can be physical, verbal or both. Its use is primarily in the area of avoidance conditioning. A dog is taught to perform tasks to avoid consequences that arise from nonperformance.

Teaching Relationship

The static exercises (Sit, Lie Down, Stand, Stay) generally are taught through varying degrees of compulsion accented by drive. Dynamic work (heeling, come here, retrieving, etc.) is taught through drive reinforced by compulsion.

Praise, Correction and Consistency

Praise and correction, equatable to drive and compulsion, are two basic ways of allowing a dog to discover, ". . . where his own advantage or disadvantage lies."* Together with commands, praise and correction

*Col. Konrad Most, *Training Dogs—A Manual* (London: Popular Dogs Publishing Co., 1954), p. 28.

comprise our elemental training language with canines. Apply each consistently so your friend can learn that his actions result in praise for the desired responses and correction for those you do not want. The person who responds inconsistently not only wastes time and effort but confounds his dog in the process.

'Cause You Got the Power

Praise and correction contribute equally to defining your status as leader. It's perhaps more apparent how corrections achieve that result: A human physically overpowers a canine, thereby asserting dominance. Praise accomplishes the same end, although how that occurs may be less obvious at first. That you give praise implies you are rightfully in a capacity of approval. It denotes that you occupy an authoritative position; that you're the leader.

Similar but Different

Praise is affirmation. It's applause. It says, "Yes, dog, that's right, and you did it very well." It's petting calmly and gently, preferably under the muzzle (to teach pooch to keep his head up), while speaking quietly. Your voice should remain constant (but not be a monotone), not becoming appreciably louder or higher-pitched.

Just as anger and rejection have no place in correction, affection and acceptance are not inherent components of praise. True, affection and acceptance creep into the approval process somewhat, but both should be given a dog throughout his life. He shouldn't have to work for them.

Correction is pressure instantly applied for an imprecise response born of active or passive resistance. It says, "You know that's not right." It's denial, not rejection; disapproval, not anger. I can't tell you I've never lost my temper when correcting a dog. I can tell you I've never seen such a lapse work in a positive sense.

Lower your voice slightly during correction to prevent the act from degenerating into an emotional contest. A quieter voice during pressure causes a dog to strain to listen rather than to concentrate on resisting.

Physical Praise

Petting is a form of communication that some dominant dogs have to learn to accept. From our perspective, such touching represents approval and intimacy. To what the professional calls a "strong dog," petting can symbolize domination, nothing more.

Reinforce Through Affirmation

Verbally praise according to what your pet has done, as in, "Good Sit," "Good Bring," "Good Stay," and so forth. This allows pooch to hear the command again (for memorization purposes) in the most positive tones you can use, thereby accenting the basis of approval.

Don't praise, "Good boy," "Good dog," "Good Fido," and the like. The animal didn't do a boy, a dog or himself, so avoid confusion that can result from inserting superfluous words. Besides, he's already a good dog. He always will be. That's not to be decided from moment to moment. Furthermore, in the technical sense, to refer to a dog as a boy or a girl is anthropomorphic. Indulging in such thinking can subtly color perspective and the messages one sends.

Praise Can Overpower

Avoid looming over your companion when praising and don't pound on him as a form of affection. The dog is not a human; nor is he a bass drum. Some folks insist, "Oh, but he likes it." Really? Watch his eyes sometime. He doesn't like it. He's learned to put up with it. (See *Learned-helplessness syndrome* in the Glossary.) Pet with a calm, medium-to-light touch. Dogs feel such contact deeply. Pounding can desensitize, much as a constantly loud voice can lose significance, eventually to become ignored.

Praise Can Be Shared

An effective manner of praise is—with the dog present—telling another person (preferably a family member) how well your pal just did a particular piece of work. Simplify the reporting, using only the animal's name, the commands to which he responded, and the praise word "Good."

For instance, if your dog, Babe, performed some particularly fine retrieving, you could walk him or her to a family member, and excitedly recite, "Babe Good Bring!" Your partner (whom you clued beforehand) should enthusiastically reply, "Babe Good Bring?" to which you reaffirm, "Babe Good Bring!" You could continue with "Babe Good Sit!"

A judicious method of praising an animal you suspect of being disposed toward taking an opportune shot at the handler. Your elbow and forearm block the jaw, and their proximity helps sense any untoward movement, thereby providing sufficient warning and time to reflexively push the animal from you.

(an element of formal retrieving). Your helper should echo, "Babe Good Sit?" to which you reply, "Babe Good Sit!"

Use of the animal's name and of the commands coupled with "Good" is half of this technique. Your approving tone of voice and that of your assistant's is the other half.

It Depends on the Particular Dog

Praise according to your pet's personality. With some this means letting the animal know the Sit he did was not only a fine Sit but was quite possibly the greatest Sit in recorded history. Other canines might see such fall-all-over-yourself effusiveness as patronizing. Like correction, praise must be tailored to each dog's capacity for absorption. "One size fits all" doesn't get it, whether discussing praise, corrections or training methods.

Extravagant praise can actually intimidate a sensitive animal, while weakly praising a strong dog can engender distrust. Dominant animals often react to gushy, syrup-mouthed approval with "I know I'm doing it well. You just hold up your end, sport."

A corresponding notion is that for some canines, usually those that are both touch insensitive and dominant, praise can be absence of correction. For others, normally the temperamentally soft, insecure animals, lack of praise can represent correction.

Lest Ye Divert

Like any communicative technique, too much praise can break the moment. When overdone, it can actually distract concentration from the business at hand. Once you've shown approval, get back to work. Like correction, praise should not be dwelt on. Don't chop off the moment; let it fade.

A Not-So-Obvious Purpose

A less realized praise function is that of controlling attention during gaps between the moving exercises (heeling, come to me, and such). When one or both of you are in motion, pooch is more likely to maintain handler awareness. He's learned that it serves his interests to do so. When the two of you are stationary, attention can more easily wander, but praise is there to hold his focus.

A Gray Aspect of Praise and Correction

I think you'll agree that praising comes more naturally than corrections. Anyone who reacts positively to a dog will pet it and otherwise communicate fondness for it. Correction, on the other hand, is a comparatively foreign action. While many have experience in disciplining a canine, some training-manual techniques are unfamiliar. Therein lies a two-pronged trap.

The first of these is obvious: that a trainer will blow the correction, either through faulty timing, improper use or mechanical error. This is the lesser problem area, however, because while it's true that a beginning handler will make his or her share of mistakes during the learning process, it's equally true that dogs are forgiving creatures by nature. The occasional inept correction won't subvert a sound training program.

The greater danger is that a trainer will concentrate on the mechanics and principles of corrections to the exclusion of contact with the dog. He'll operate on or against his friend rather than with him. A person can concentrate on a given act to such a degree that while execution of the action may appear flawless, communication is nonexistent. In that setting, it's as though the trainer is operating at a psychic distance from his pet, even though he's physically within inches of the animal.

The solutions? First, realize that correcting a dog—like any skill—must be learned. Mistakes are a by-product of learning. They happen. Rather than chide yourself after an error, be glad you're aware that you did goof and learn from the experience. Realize where you went wrong, analyze what triggered the mistake and try not to repeat it. Second—and like all abstracts, this is a foggy area—study your pal's reactions to pressure. There's a discernible attitudinal difference between the dog that responds with an air of "Egad! You must mean what you say" versus a response of "What was that for? Why are you abusing me? Who or what are you becoming?" Like praise, corrections must be intimate, or they teach only distance.

Correction: Rule Number 1

Here's as close as I'll get to giving you a hard-and-fast rule: Never use your pet's name during correction. Doing so risks that the animal may misinterpret the meaning: that you feel he, rather than his behavior is no good.

Correction: The Basis

One and only one circumstance justifies correction: contention—when a dog says, "I choose to defy you!" Force is then a legitimate response, saying, "Think again!" In that sense, correction is a teaching tool: It delineates options. Mild, suggestive force is sometimes a teaching necessity, but using untoward compulsion to demonstrate a lesson is abuse, nothing more.

It follows, then, that the answer to "Why are corrections needed?" is "to avoid future need for correction; so that once the dog understands the alternatives, force is no longer needed."

How Fast?

Though novices often ask how forcefully to correct, proper technique should be concerned with "How quickly?" before "How hard?" The optimal time to correct is when pooch is a split second into a disobedient act, when he's "thinking" about violating a directive, so to speak. Correction (or praise) more than two or three seconds after the fact is ineffective.

Besides, correction at the earliest possible stage requires less force than would be needed otherwise. Some feel it's preferable to let a dog commit a disobedient act in its entirety so that "you can really get on him." Such dim logic is attributable to the fact that some folks can't read canine intent.

The Rule of Minimal Toughness

Equated in sheer force, be one inch tougher than the dog; no more, no less. While trainers determine what is to be taught, dogs set the limits of how much force is needed to reinforce. Accordingly, the lightest correction that does the job is the proper one. A correction applied harder than needed can teach, yes, but what it teaches is fear of the leader.

Common Sense

Never correct a frightened or confused dog. The result is heightened fear or confusion. A canine in either state concentrates on survival, not on learning. Corrections in such an instance are abuse, teaching only fear and distrust.

Not as Long as He's Trying

Corrections have no application when a dog is trying to do right. A contradictory attitude teaches a canine to lose. Such backward thinking says, "There's no point in trying." It also implies the unrealistic expectation that a dog can or should perform any exercise perfectly from day one. Were that the case, practice would be a meaningless term.

Get on with It

Don't dwell on a correction (except in response to aggression toward you). Apply it quickly and move on. Grudges serve no useful purpose; patience, understanding and forgiveness do.

Correction Versus Abuse

A definite yet hazy line exists between effectuating control and stripping a dog of his identity, his senses of initiative, creativity and spontaneity. Some canines accept human regulation without forfeiture of self, even when the force required is considerable. Others wilt under the slightest pressure. Of course, such dogs are at opposite ends of the continuum. Most are spaced between the extremes.

The aforementioned line is wavy, not straight. In some circumstances, more pressure can be exerted with less risk of imposing stifling, inhibiting censorship. In other situations, marginal force can knock down an otherwise strong dog. You must learn to read your best friend, to assess his strength in this regard. No one can do it for you. My best service is to make you aware that this canine tendency exists and advise you to err toward caution when using force.

Correction Level

Build up on corrections, making them progressively tougher until you determine what it takes to run your pet; then stay at that level. Better one should initially undercorrect than overcorrect. It's preferable to correct twice at first, while you're getting the feel of your dog, than it is to frighten through excessive force. Bear in mind, you can always raise the ante.

Consistency in Corrections

Once you've determined what it takes to say, "Oh, yes, you will!" (or, "Oh, no, you won't!") don't retreat from that degree of force. To consistently undercorrect is an exercise in cruelty; it promises more and tougher corrections later. This is because continually underdone force makes a tough animal tougher. It makes him more resistant by stiffening his resolve and desensitizing his neck, ultimately leading to sterner measures than would have been required had initial force been commensurate with temperament.

They're Not Created Equal

Within most litters, much disparity exists in terms of touch sensitivity and in dominant and submissive tendencies. A dirty look is all the correction some can handle; others bring visions of a wrecking ball to mind.

Size Is Not Equatable with Toughness

Big doesn't imply toughness; little doesn't presuppose fragility. The Alaskan Malamute shown here is a pussycat. I've known more than one Miniature Schnauzer that could dominate him with a glance.

Make It Clear

There's a school of thought that holds that corrections should be made unaccompanied by verbal remonstrations. While rare instances exist where that style of correction is proper, the silent-correction mode is a trap.

True, your pet can't understand every word you say, but he comprehends intent more fully if you vocalize displeasure. Giving *brief* voice to your purpose leads to better communication. Furthermore, the day will come when you won't praise for every action—you don't want to spend your life praising for obedience learned years ago. Thus, if corrections are always applied in silence, a dog can learn to associate displeasure with your lack of verbal response to proper behavior.

One or the Other

In keeping with the foregoing, when correcting a dog physically, don't lay a prolonged speech on him. There can be words, yes, but not

Buddies.

a sermon. At the same time, when getting after a canine verbally—one of those tirades that begins with "Now let me tell you just how things are going to be . . ."—it's seldom best to accompany the marching orders with pronounced force.

Avoid the Windmill Syndrome

Corrections should entail as little handler movement as possible. Excessive motion can tell a dog that the trainer has difficulty handling him physically. With the more sensitive animal, protracted handler motion can add the undesirable element of fear to an otherwise instructive correction. This is because some dogs are sensitive to sudden motion. Also, exorbitant handler gyrations tend to distract from the business at hand. The dog is more concerned with the trainer's atypical movements than with the lesson.

A Myth About Corrections and Praise

Many trainers tie correction and praise together improperly. For example, a dog that knows Sit doesn't respond to the command. The handler corrects the animal and then immediately praises for sitting. The theory is that such methodology demonstrates the dog's alternative—respond to command and receive praise or be forced to respond and then receive praise. This is one of those notions that works better on paper than in practice. To praise a dog for not responding to known commands makes as much sense as correcting him for responding to known commands.

The dog didn't sit; the trainer forced him to sit. Approval should be given for things a dog does, not for things that he is pressured to do. Praise is celebration, and it could seem to a dog that a postcorrection "celebration" is due to the fact that the animal received physical force. He could wonder, "What are you so happy about? I didn't do anything. You did, but I didn't."

In the foregoing example, a more sensible sequence is as follows. The trainer commands, "Sit"; the dog refuses. The trainer instantly corrects the animal into position. After two or three seconds, the dog is moved a few steps and is again commanded, "Sit." This time pooch responds correctly and *this time* is praised, "Good Sit." Now the praise fits the response; it makes sense.

The Carryover Principle

Like praise, corrections can have a useful slide-over effect. Consider the following illustration:

A trainer is working a particularly large or tough dog and is having difficulty correcting the animal for refusing to lie down. The dog understands the command—he simply won't comply. Let's also stipulate that the canine is familiar with the dual concept of Heeling and Automatic Sit. (Heeling requires a dog to Sit, without verbal command, next to the trainer whenever the trainer stops walking.) Keeping in mind that most people can more easily apply a forceful Sit correction than they can a Lie Down correction, because of the leverage required, the trainer commands, "Heel." The first time that the animal fails to sit automatically, or does so slowly, he is corrected with appreciable force (but relative to size and temperament, of course) and is immediately commanded to lie down. More often than not, the Sit correction's influence carries into the next exercise, causing the dog to forgo resistance to the Lie Down command, and he goes to ground without argument.

An Exception

Corrections are sometimes better delayed than instantly applied. For example, when teaching heeling, should a dog break from my side, I normally correct at the first misstep. However, if I know or even suspect the animal has a proclivity to bite in response to pressure, I allow him to move away a few steps before applying force. My thought is, should the dog respond to compulsion by reflexively wheeling about and snapping, good old me is out of harm's way. The short distance also affords me reaction time should the animal push the issue.

Don't Lose What You've Got

Sometimes a correction is theoretically in order but is better passed by. Consider a situation in which you and your charge have been training for several minutes and he's been doing very, very well. Then his attention wanders momentarily, resulting in a marginal error. That's not the time to apply a physical correction. To do so would send a message signed Simon Legree, risking a dampening of ardor for obedience with you. The example is especially applicable to the animal that has been in training for only a few weeks. In this case, it's better to apply a moderate verbal remonstration and repeat the exercise so that the dog can do it right.

Hard-core folks disagree with the point, demanding perfection at all times. I respect their sincerity, if not their judgment. Such expectations are unrealistic and are therefore unreasonable. No animal (least of all human ones, it should be remembered) operates flawlessly, and the concept of an "honest mistake" is valid.

Appropriate Corrections

When correcting a dog, be certain that it's for the right reasons. For instance, let's say you're working pooch near other dogs. Should he attempt to lunge away for purposes of engaging another for fight or play, the correction should include the message that the force is for leaving you or for breaking the command he was then under, not for attempting to go after another dog. Should the animal you're heeling attempt to jump at another, correct yours for broken heeling, not for whatever motivation he had in leaving you.

The reason is, it's simply easier for a dog to learn a positive than a negative. As that's in keeping with canine nature, it's therefore more comprehensible for a dog to learn to do than it is to learn not to do.

Improper Corrections

Two so-called corrections have received wide circulation in recent years. The first concerns striking an aggressive dog across the muzzle with a length of rubber hose, sometimes having first inserted a piece of wooden dowel therein.

Leave the hose in the garden where it belongs. Not only can such a blow cause head shyness; it risks accidentally striking an eye. I once saw a self-proclaimed expert, whose aim was on a par with his breed knowledge, nearly blind a purportedly aggressive Sheltie whose first-week-obedience-class sin was barking playfully at another dog.

The second out-of-line correction is commonly referred to as hanging the dog, which I've witnessed for infractions no greater than a slow Sit. It's applied by literally suspending a canine off the ground via the leash/choke collar until the animal changes his ways or passes out. Such "technique" constitutes criminal abuse. It has no place in everyday training. Its only justifiable use is handler protection, and even then only when one has no other out. I've resorted to it as a defense three times since 1976, and each occurrence was triggered by a dog whose objective (and who had the means) was to put me in the hospital.

The Shift Between Correction and Understanding

Correction frequency decreases as canine understanding increases. While this states the obvious, most trainers have known dogs that had been in training for years but were still being corrected for basic infractions—even though the animals had earned obedience titles! The education, while it may have been sufficient for the animals to "clumsy" their way through a rigid and unchanging ring routine, was incomplete in that they were never shown to totally appreciate their obligations.

The truly sad part is that the canines mentioned were seldom corrected properly in the past, which led to their having to be inordinately pressured in the present. Once a sound dog understands, he does what's required. *Canis familiaris* is just too intelligent to be thought of otherwise.

Praise, Correction and . . .

Deflection was first mentioned when speaking about gender conflicts (chapter 3, "Pretraining and Bonding"). It's a helpful technique for situations in which neither praise nor correction seems appropriate but some type of action is called for.

Deflection is problem solving through circumvention. It's overlooking low-risk contention or peripheral negative behavior to prevent either from mushrooming. The following account imparts the concept's essence.

A Dog Is Not a Side of Beef

Some years ago, while helping to position a student's Akita in the Stand-Stay (remain motionless in a standing position), the animal turned toward me and growled. I deflectively muttered, "The same to you," and continued with the business at hand, seeming to ignore him. I could have overpowered the dog and might have were he mine. However, the Akita is a breed that, like many, prefers one master, and this animal's resentment was on the order of "Who do you think you are to be putting hands on me?" He simply didn't appreciate a stranger's domination. For all I know, he found my brand of mouthwash objectionable as well.

A canine has the right to choose the people he feels comfortable around, just as you and I do. So long as a dog doesn't attempt to climb my frame, I deflect lesser signs of displeasure.

IN GENERAL

"In This Corner . . ."

Don't roughhouse with your pet, especially if he is of the larger breeds. Doing so may appear harmless and cute during puppyhood, but later it can backfire tragically. Such "play" can teach that contention against you is acceptable behavior.

A Little Consideration, Please

Don't laugh at a dog. Derision hurts him. Laughing *with* him is fine, in the sense of sharing an enjoyable moment, but never *at*. He's been provided for your amazement, not amusement. Those who ridicule a canine only reveal their distance from him.

Not Unless You Think He'll Answer You

Along similar lines, don't ask a dog questions. A pack leader doesn't ask; he or she directs. Furthermore, when a person queries a canine, the common reaction is anxiety. This is for three reasons: First, the dog is immediately put at a disadvantage: He can't participate. That is, do you honestly expect an answer? Second, you're saying you don't understand. To wit, should your pet limp to you, he's already shown you what's wrong. Questions would signify imperceptiveness on your part. Third, a questioning tone imparts uncertainty. The dog is no friend of indecision; it only heightens nervousness.

So Much for Unisex

Tendencies exist among trainers. Female handlers often overpraise and undercorrect. Male trainers often tend to be just the opposite: strong on corrections and stingy with praise. Neither extreme is conducive to bonding. No, these traits don't constitute an absolute truth, merely an observation. Exceptions always exist. The intent is only to suggest, to quote the bard: "Know thyself."

Uses of Food

The proper use of food is neither as bribe nor as reward. Once pooch understands that your commands must be obeyed, an occasional tidbit following a Recall ("Come to me"), for example, is permissible. However, present the snack not as a bonus but as a gift between friends: "Why, look what I just happened to find in my pocket—have some." In the foregoing example, your pet's reward is that coming to you allows him to be with you.

Absolutes

Having told you of these various rules and concepts, remember that few absolutes exist in the world of training. Some techniques are merely more effective than others more often than not. During seminars, I've often exhorted the assemblage, "Now, here's one thing you hardly ever want to do," referring to a particular training aspect. Then, moments after making that statement, I occasionally find myself *doing* that very thing because the dog with whom I was working and the situation called for it. Similarly, I've instructed classes, "This is how you do that," and then applied the technique differently two minutes later for the same reason: I saw that the dog would learn more easily when taught a particular point via a method other than the one I normally use.

A professional, regardless of preferences as to what's right and wrong in the world of canine training, is eclectic in his or her approach to each dog. He or she is flexible and does whatever it takes to produce a reliable, confident, happy worker.

Not Even Mine

This you may take to the bank: There is no perfect training method, no single correct or foolproof approach for teaching each and every dog each and every exercise.

That accounts for the proliferation of books on the subject. Were there an ideal method, there'd be a single obedience text instead of the many currently in print. This fact lends support to the earlier thesis that training is far more art than science, just as art is more interpretation than definition. Experience with those who claim that their way is the only way suggests that such folks have spent too much time on the Mount.

Reflection

A handler always ends up with the dog he deserves.

Royal Air Force Dog Training School

SECTION II

Companion Obedience

6

Basic Tools

LEASHES

You're going to need some equipment. First there's the matter of a leash, which should measure four to six feet. Later, you'll need a fifteen- to twenty-foot lead, but for now the shorter leash is adequate.

Preferred Leash Types and Sizes

The criterion for the correct leash and snap is, the lighter the better, but nothing your pet could break. Using too heavy a lead can distract attention from the handler, redirecting it toward the equipment. Of course, that would interfere with a basic goal: attracting focus toward you.

For largest breeds, use a leather lead of five-eighths to three-fourths inch in width. For Labrador Retriever–sized dogs, a leather or webbed-cotton leash one-half to five-eighths inch wide is best. For the Springer Spaniel range, a webbed-cotton lead, three-eighths to one-half inch in width is adequate. For smaller canines, a show lead with a light clasp handles well.

Nonrecommended Types

Chain leashes are not only rough on hands and legs; they're point-lessly heavy. Also, chain leads are noisy, which lessens canine motivation to concentrate on the trainer. Since the animal can hear where the leash is—that is, where you are—he has less need to work at keeping track of you.

Nylon leashes can also cause problems. They can quickly generate remarkable friction, and should a large, powerful dog lunge away, burn ointment for the hands may be needed.

COLLARS

Time for Some Suspended Disbelief

If you've seen a pinch collar (also known as a prong or German collar) but lack experience with one, its appearance may have put you off, understandably. There're no two ways about it: They're god-awful looking contraptions. A novice's first reaction may be emotional rather than rational: "Not with my dog!" Such a response is as commendable from the standpoint of caring and concern as it is totally unreasonable. A pinch collar is a far kinder piece of equipment than a choke collar. True, a pinch collar's appearance is not unlike that of torture-catalog items—by comparison, a choke collar "looks" friendly—but this is a classic case of what you see is *not* what you get.

Keep in mind that we're training a dog, not a human. A pinch collar's function is to put teeth on the neck of an animal that instinctively knows more about that kind of sensation than you and I could intellectualize in a month. Watch a dam as she disciplines a pup. You'll see the young one instantly calm in response to the feel of mom's teeth on its neck. By the way, no, a pinch collar won't poke holes in a dog. Such is possible, I suppose, but I'd think a person would have to work at it.

When using a pinch collar—which I think of as a "tooth collar," for the reasons stated—far fewer corrections are needed than if a choker were used. Once a canine realizes what he's up against, he works harder at business and less at resistance. The animal errs a good deal less, thereby requiring fewer applications of force. The less negative reinforcement (force) used, the more positive is the training session. Furthermore, since a pinch collar is an easier device for a beginner to use effectively, he or she is less likely to do little more than toughen a dog's neck—and his resolve.

Skill with a choke collar develops only after much experience. The typical novice can do little more than throttle with one. Contrarians should ponder why the device is called a *choke* collar in the first place. For a canine, the sensation of being choked can easily induce panic. It would

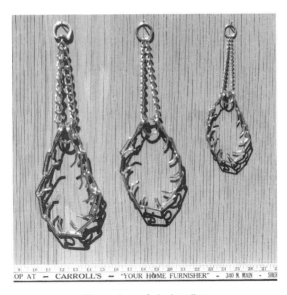

Three sizes of pinch collars.

A pinch collar worn incorrectly (*left*) and correctly (*right*). Notice the collar on the left contains too many links to be effective.

be a rare occurrence for a dog to be choked in the wild, his natural setting. Because the feeling of suffocation is foreign to his experience, he has no notion as to how to deal with it. He was born with scant instinctive knowledge about coping with such a sensation except to resist its source— you. A dog thus threatened doesn't concentrate on learning but on moment-to-moment survival.

Dogs are carelessly killed every day by owners who leave choke collars on unattended pets that caught the collar on something. It is unheard of for a pinch collar to strangle; moreover, a trainer is more likely to remove such equipment after a session.

Still skeptical? An experiment you may care to try (at your own risk) is fitting one of the two types of collars around your left thigh and the other around your right. Yank—don't merely pull—each collar forcefully several times. Tomorrow, no signs of abuse will be apparent where the pinch collar was. The other leg, where the choker was, will be black and blue. This demonstration alone should make the point.

A Caution

Training collars—pinch or choke—can elicit a combative response, especially when used with so-called fighting breeds. A closable collar on the ''wrong'' dog can stimulate that canine into an attack frame of mind before you can blink. With such an animal, muzzling is a sound option.

Pinch-Collar Sizes

Pinch collars are commonly available in three link sizes: small, medium and large. The larger the link, the greater the biting surface. The small collar is for dogs up to the size of a small Doberman. The medium-link size is for any other canine, except for the largest breeds, for which the large-linked collar is appropriate. If your pet is small for the breed, use a collar one size smaller than that suggested. With a dog that seems impervious to the size recommended, use the next-larger model.

Fitting a Pinch Collar

A loosely worn pinch collar is not only ineffective; it can fly apart. Attach it snugly (though not excruciatingly tight) so that it appears to stand around the neck. Unlike the choke, pinch-collar length can be adjusted by removing or adding links.

A choke collar worn incorrectly (*left*) and correctly (*right*).

Don't do it! This collar has been shortened by hitching the correct link without removing the excess links, a practice that can cause the collar to come apart when leash pressure is applied.

An example of too much collar for the dog. Note how this oversized device rests near the animal's shoulders.

Choke Collars

If you still feel more comfortable using a choke, keep a few thoughts in mind. The proper length for a chain choke is equal to the circumference of the neck, plus two or three inches. Link size is dependent on the animal's size: Large for the largest breeds, medium for those in the German Shepherd range, small for spaniel types and very small for those tinier than a Sheltie.

A choke collar is worn with the *live ring* (which makes the collar contract—the other is called the *dead ring*, which the collar passes through) coming over the top of the neck toward you when pooch is facing forward at your left side.* Attaching your lead to the live ring allows the collar to release once a tightened leash is relaxed.

Electronic Collars

While I neither own nor use such devices, these collars are handy in special situations (excessive barking, chasing game or livestock etc.). My objection to shock collars for fundamental training is that I want my dog to know that all praise and correction flow from me. I don't wish to take the chance he might conclude that an unnamed force zapped him!

If shock collars already have a useful place in your program, fine. I'll never tell you to fight success. Should such equipment have appeal but be new to your experience, allow your pet to wear the apparatus for a week or so prior to activation. Just before working the dog, slip a leather (or cloth) collar onto his neck. The animal will be more likely to associate any corrections with the leather collar because he will have been wearing it for a briefer time. The result is an obedient canine even when he wears a normal collar. Were you to put on an electronic collar and apply a correction soon thereafter, pooch would likely relate the sensation to the equipment. This could result in conditional obedience: the dog minding only when adorned with the device.

Reflection

You want a friend in this life? Get a dog!

President Harry S Truman

*The general position described above is termed the Heel position. Should you choose to teach heeling at your right side, reverse the collar placement.

86

7

Fundamental Lessons

A CCOMPANIED by each element's command, *Dog Logic*'s Companion Obedience program is outlined below:

Sit   Sit and remain sitting until commanded otherwise.

Fuss   1. Maintain the Heel position, sitting automatically (without spoken command) when the person halts.

       2. Return to the Heel position and Sit.

Stay   Remain exactly where you are, in your present posture.

Platz Lie down and Stay until commanded otherwise.

Hup   Jump over, through or onto the designated obstacle.

Here Sit facing the handler, after coming to him or her.

Wait Stand and Stay until commanded otherwise.

Good Praise word, used to communicate approval.

No   Cease what you are doing, now and for all time.

Later Do whatever you want (within reason).

Command Preferences

Fuss and Platz are German terms. Fuss means "foot" and rhymes with "loose." Platz translates as "spot," or "place," and rhymes with "lots."

Command selection is not arbitrary. Fuss is better than the conventional Heel to avoid a soundalike with the Recall (come to me) command Here. Also, because Fuss is a foreign word, it makes a stranger's walking off with your pet more difficult.

To circumvent any negative preconditioning, Platz is preferable to the common Down. By the time many canines are started in obedience, they've learned that Down means to get off something or someone. Too often a dog has also learned to ignore the command. Rather than teach, "Down used to mean one thing but now means something else," and that compliance, which was optional, is now mandatory; it's simply easier for trainer and dog to start afresh with a new word. Besides, Down can cause confusion because many words are similar sounding: town, sound, round etc.

Here is preferable to the traditional Come. The pitch of many people's voices causes Come, with its harsh "Kuh" sound, to communicate unmeant illusions of anger or impatience. This is especially true when the command must be given loudly, as when one's pet is far away. Hostility is the wrong message to send when calling a dog.

Wait is more advantageous than the conventional Stand. After learning Sit, some dogs react so quickly when hearing the "S" sound (as in, "Stand") that their rears are halfway to the Sit position before the handler can complete the word. To teach a slowed response to differentiate between similar-sounding commands is to instill hesitancy and nervousness.

Regardless of command preferences, two that should not be used concurrently are Down and Come. They can sound alike to a canine, especially over long distances or in noisy settings. Ring trainers can get away with using both because they're dealing with rigid and unchanging obedience standards. The real world offers few such patterns to cue on, however, and I've seen more than one otherwise reliable street dog confuse Down with Come.

Release Cue

The release-cue concept is likely new for beginning trainers. It supposedly communicates that a dog may "take five." The handler won't be giving commands for a while; therefore, the animal is on his own. On paper, it sounds like a good idea. In practice, it's less so.

I don't wish to ever tell my dog that I have neither purpose nor time for him. That would contradict my training ideology, for it suggests there are times when we aren't us. Such a notion is fallacious in canine terms—a pack never stops being a pack: It's always on simmer. Like the dog's perception of the world around him, it is absolute.

Furthermore, many trainers employ a release cue in a manner that communicates a sense of rejoicing that the session is at an end. The obedience they've been doing is finished at last, thank God! I've seen many dogs perform with an air of drudgery until a release was given, at which time there was dancing in the streets. Such an attitude is exactly backward: Happiness should be shared at the start of and during each session, not because it's ended.

However, those accustomed to using a release prompt may be uncomfortable without one. A better cue than the prevalent Okay is Later. Okay is too ingrained in our speech habits to be a wise choice. It's too easy for a handler to use it unintentionally and not be aware of having done so. More than once I've known a trainer to comment "Okay" to an acquaintance and then correct his or her pet for alleged sudden disobedience.

Other Lessons

Tracking is properly deferred for now. Since heeling teaches a dog to keep his head up, while tracking requires that the nose be down, it's preferable to concentrate on one mode or the other during initial lessons. Protection work can be ongoing, and retrieving may be started during the third week, but not if pooch is having difficulty with any novice exercises.

Get the Feel of it First

If you've little or no training experience, be aware that some techniques require more than marginal agility, timing and coordination. Before implementing a new procedure, think it through and practice it without your companion nearby. The time to discover you're having difficulty with an unfamiliar maneuver is not when the dog is present and enjoying the show. It's not only bad form, but one might feel frustration and anger under such pressure and could vent such feelings against pooch.

Work Versus Play

The following overview covers the first few weeks of formal obedience training. Remember that the program allows for playtime as well as for teaching. Also, at this beginning level, do *not* give any obedience commands during play periods. Later, after a dog has learned much, it'll be proper to intersperse commands among playful moments, but to do so prematurely could lessen enjoyment of playtime.

Training Outline—Obedience I
(5 weeks)

Exercise	1	2	3	4	5
Heel and Auto-Sit	On lead	Mild distracts	Increase distracts	As needed	Distraction proofing
Sit-Stay	6 feet / 1 minute	15 feet / 2 minutes	25 feet / 3 minute signal	Handler out of sight 1 minute	Handler out of sight 2 minutes
Down-Stay		15 feet / 2 minutes	25 feet / 3 minute signal	Handler out of sight 1 minute	Handler out of sight 3 minutes
Jumping			At heel low height	At heel med height	At heel higher
Recall			6 feet	15 feet	25 feet
Finish				Teach	With recall
Stand-Stay					6 feet / 20 seconds

Reflection

I am called a dog because I fawn on those who give me anything, I yelp at those who refuse, and I set my teeth in rascals.

Diogenes

8

First Week

_____

Pacing

The following five chapters cover training weeks one through five. However, it may be that your pet should be accelerated or slowed in the lessons. That's a determination only you can make. As a guide, most canines can deal with new material every fourth day. Also, some days pooch is more receptive to new lessons than at other times. Referred to as *teachable moments*, those are periods when it seems that you can't teach fast enough. If at any point you sense your pal is ready to advance, even though seven calendar days haven't lapsed, get on with it. No good purpose is served by courting boredom. Conversely, if a routine causes difficulty, slow up until your companion is comfortable with the work.

FIRST DAY

Collar On

Begin by adorning your pet with the pinch collar mentioned in chapter 6, "Basic Tools," positioning it with the chain portion at the back of the neck. Be sure the links aren't pinning ears. Attach the six-foot leash to the collar's uppermost ring and walk your companion to the training area (which, I'm assuming, is less than fifty feet away. If it's farther, use a noncontractible belt-and-buckle collar for the journey.).

Your attitude should be that there's very little that pooch can do wrong. Don't expect correct deportment yet—it's not been taught. If the dog pulls against the leash or even attempts to drag you along—some will, even when wearing a pinch collar—endure such antics for the moment.

An alternative way to initiate this first day is to greet the animal with "Hi. I'm Alpha. You aren't. Care to argue the point?" But that's a lousy beginning. It's a negative approach to a positive being. Better your friend should be glad to see you coming next time. You can always overpower the dog, if need be, but it's healthier to save that ace (which may never be needed) than to play it in your opening hand. Besides, this brief trek affords time to reevaluate any conclusions about your pet's strength, coordination, predispositions and state of mind.

Don't allow leash chewing, however. That's a bad habit to get started. Not only does a lead cost a few dollars; it's an extension of the handler (i.e., you could be next). Leash gnawing can be inhibited by a firm "No," accompanied by an open-handed smack under the chin.

Question: "How hard do I swat?"

Answer: "How tough is your dog?"

Corrections should entail the minimal force necessary to get the job done. A trainer can always get tougher. In any case, a few seconds after any disciplining, follow with a quick pat on the neck and the word "Good" to demonstrate you haven't taken a dislike to the animal.

The "Bonkers" Syndrome

Some dogs rebel against leash-and-collar restraint, performing amazing contortions in the process. No cause for concern exists as long as pooch is reacting from a sense of being thwarted. He'll soon cease gyrations without coaching. Should he carry on such that you feel he needs assistance in settling, help him, either through petting and soft talking or firmness and admonition, depending on the animal's personality.

Occasionally, a dog is encountered whose initial response to leash and collar is outright panic. He reacts with terror, as though he can't understand what's taken hold of him. Force isn't the answer in that situation—pressuring an already frightened canine only spooks him further. To calm a fearful dog, gentle petting and soft words are usually best, as is kneeling nearby to eliminate any towering image. Draw his focus to you and to the fact he has an understanding, caring friend who

Correct leash grip.

can be trusted. Once your pal settles, entice and encourage by patting your leg as you continue the journey.

Once You Arrive at the Training Area

The first educational objective is to establish certain basic concepts in your pet's mind as rapidly as he can absorb them. Primary among these is that you are benevolently in charge. Toward this end, when you arrive at the training site, capture pooch's best attention. Until he's listening, he isn't able to hear you. That is, the first thing you must say is that you have things to say.

Remember, at this stage your pet has no inkling of what's happening. You do, but he doesn't. How could he? A dog isn't capable of reviewing a course outline. Thus, it's best to start with an action that quickly gains attention and provides control.

From dog to dog, concentration varies from a condition of total handler fixation to not being present at the situation. As a trainer, you must quickly and accurately assess capacity so as not to demand too much or too little. In most instances, focus is secured quickly with minimal effort through leash taming.

LEASH TAMING

The concept discussed in this section is often referred to as "leash breaking." However, since it's not our intent to break anything—leash or spirit—the term "leash taming" is preferable.

Leash Grip

The right hand is preferable for leash control, but the left may initially seem easier. Using whichever hand you prefer, put your thumb through the hand loop, positioning said loop's curve just behind the knuckle. Close your fingers around the loop, thereby enveloping it (but not your thumb) in a fist. Even the largest dog can't pull a leash held thus from the hand. Hold excess slack with fingertips of the same hand.

Technique

After you've arrived at the training site, pooch may want to pull you along as he checks things out. That's normal: A dog finding himself in a new area typically proceeds to sniff and otherwise explore every square foot thereof. Occasionally, he air scents, but more often he has his beak close to the ground. This is natural: His nose is far more acute than his eyes or ears. Since you'll soon be teaching the concept of heeling, and given that no dog can heel and track simultaneously, this is the first behavior to address. In the process of altering this canine tendency of "Now, you keep up with me, y'hear?" you'll also gain attention.

As the dog begins to walk (trot, run, gallop) away in quest of things sniffable, release any slack you've been holding and brace yourself. *Immediately after* pooch reaches the lead's end, with a degree of force commensurate with his mass and velocity, walk in the direction opposite the one he took. If he went north, you go south. In turning around, he should see your retreating back. While a dog ultimately learns that correction, like praise, comes from the handler, for now it's better that he thinks the jolt was a product of circumstance; that it was caused by your decision to change course, not by a contrived action. A dog could mistakenly interpret the latter as belittlement of self instead of the lesson intended: Since you change direction without warning, he'd best keep his eyes on you.

After reaching the end of the lead, pooch may run in your direction and past you, only to hit the end of the leash again. As before, reverse your travel 180 degrees just after he does so. When he next nears you, a smiled "Hi, pup" is proper. So is patting your leg, encouraging him to join you. Follow this gesture by another immediate change in direction. The dog may begin to accompany you at this point. If he does, a gentle "Good" is in order, especially if he looks your way as he trots along.

Continue the procedure as needed: The dog heads east; you go west. All you're saying is that you'll allow him to hit leash's end as many times as *he* wishes—his behavior is up to him; it's his responsibility, not yours—and that anytime he tires of the consequence, he might try keeping track of where you are. The era of dragging you along as something of an inconvenience is gone. It just ended.

It's okay to repeat the gesture of encouraging pooch to accompany you, but keep it low-key. The dog must discern the wisdom of keeping his eyes on you *for and by himself*. Should you lessen the price—such as reducing the shock by moving toward the animal as he nears the lead's end—then he's calling the shots, not you. Remember, while the mechanical objective is to gain attention, the overall message is that you'll no longer facilitate or enable unacceptable behavior. Those days are history.

Long Leash?

You may be aware of an approach that utilizes a fifteen-to twenty-foot lead for leash taming. Several reasons support staying with the six-foot leash.

With a longer line, too much time passes between the instant the dog flees and the consequence. Granted, a canine will eventually associate flight with unpleasantness, but he'll do so quicker if the pressure is timed closer to the infraction. Also, using a longer leash can impair perception that force came from the trainer. When a dog is several yards away, it stands to reason he's less likely to associate stimuli as having originated with the handler. He could decide that an unknown force took hold of him. That's the stuff of which paranoia is born.

Third, when training a particularly large, powerful animal, the momentum accumulated during a twenty-foot flight can transmit sufficient force to jerk the handler out of his or her socks. Finally—and this is aimed at the first-time trainer—effective handling can be difficult even when using a short lead. It's more so when having to deal with a cumbersome fifteen- to twenty-footer.

But if Perchance . . .

Should you be working an unusually resistant or tough animal—I've met my share that, even when wearing a pinch collar, tried to drag the trainer—it may be necessary to yank the lead in the direction opposite the dog's line of travel just as he reaches its end. Remaining stationary as a canine discovers the lead is finite normally imparts sufficient force to make the point, but with a steel-necked, iron-willed animal, more pressure may be required. A powerful dog pulling directly away can seem difficult to turn, but it's easy to alter his direction simply by stepping to either side of his line of travel. This creates a 90-degree angle from which power can easily be exerted.

Allow for size and temperament. With a rock-hard Rottweiler male, for instance, you may have to put back, legs and shoulders into the correction. A forearm pop is normally sufficient for a tough Brittany Spaniel. With a resistant Cairn Terrier, a wrist flick should get the job done. In the case of a Miniature Dachshund, finger pressure typically proves adequate. The constant in each case is that all the animal should see when he turns in the direction of pressure is you walking away. The idea is still to show him that your route isn't predictable and that to avoid further unpleasantness he'd do well to monitor your whereabouts.

Formal instruction per se is not being given here, for no commands are being used. Proper schooling begins by teaching Sit. This can often be started following a few minutes of leash taming, but if more time is needed to absorb that lesson, defer teaching Sit for now. It's seldom wise to implement a step until a dog is solid on the one before it.

THE SIT

Static lessons (Sit, Stand, Lie Down) are more easily taught than active ones (Heel, Come, Jump). This is especially true for novice trainers, since a motionless animal is easier to deal with. Of the static lessons, the Sit is the easiest for most people to teach. Also, for most dogs it's the simplest traditional command to learn.

The Preface states that *Dog Logic* ''offers concepts and techniques that may not be encountered elsewhere.'' Experienced trainers may have already begun to discern this. If you're new to obedience, the following bit of history is presented as a frame of reference concerning one of the more basic elements of formal training: the Sit.

The Sit—Conventional Teaching Method

Orthodox teaching of Sit finds the trainer causing pooch to face forward at the left side and saying, ''[Dog's name], Sit!'' Coincident with the command, the trainer pulls the leash upward with the right hand while pushing the rump down with the left. While that method isn't improper or totally ineffective technique—it works, after a fashion—it's weak procedure.

The most serious detriment is it can cruelly mislead. It can say nothing more than ''Sit means I'm going to pull up on your collar and push down on your butt.'' It may not convey, ''Sit means you must assume this position.'' Moreover, inaccurately defining the dog's responsibility occurs at a most inauspicious time: during the introduction to obedience training. It can communicate a fallacious message at a critical juncture.

Thus, a major problem with teaching the Sit in the foregoing manner is that a dog often learns exactly what he's been shown: that ''Sit!'' means the trainer will do it for him through a push-pull process. This is why novices often lament, ''I've been training this dog to sit for a week now, and he still doesn't get the idea.'' In truth, the animal has gotten the idea just fine.

Moreover, when the handler gets around to compelling "Sit!" with force for noncompliance, he effectively changes the rules. He jumps from doing the dog's work to physical force without *first giving the animal a notion of the whys and the wherefores*. That's the technique's seldom-realized, cruel aspect alluded to earlier. Prior to the first correction, pooch was never given fair warning of the alternatives, which is a good way to culture resentment and distrust. It can also lead to being bitten, should one be working a canine whose inclination toward unexpected pressure is fire.

Often the push-pull approach boomerangs, too, suggesting to a dog that he should resist trainer intention. Pushing the rump of some canines only stimulates them to push back. Add to that the fact that some handlers can't compel the Sit in this manner because they lack the necessary strength. I've watched novices trying to Sit large, powerful dogs, and what transpired was low comedy: the dog bucking, whipping his body from side to side against resistible force, the owner trying to maintain position next to the animal and losing the attempt at control.

Unchecked resistance—such as that manifested by the dog that learns he can't be pushed into the Sit—can cause a session to deteriorate into a dogfight. It's self-evident that sound training policy doesn't risk imbuing resistance or contention.

With smaller canines, the technique causes the trainer to loom over the animal. This posture can be unsettling to a sensitive pooch, for it can appear that the trainer may topple onto him. Not only can that distract attention from the lesson; it can teach a dog to associate nervousness with the command.

Another problem with the method is that it requires too much handler movement, which should always be kept to a minimum. Your efforts must appear effort*less* if pooch is to perceive you as pack leader. Also, if you happen to be working unawares with the *wrong* dog, you're wide open to a potentially harmful response. The phrase "face bit" leaps to mind. Minimal pressure brings some canines to the *fight-or-flight* state.

The final drawback to this procedure is that it's a trap of showing too many things at once. It teaches Sit relative to the Heel position. While experienced trainers usually know better, novices often teach (or try to teach) the Sit in this manner, only to later correct their charges for doing the right thing in the wrong place. Showing a dog Sit and then correcting him for blowing an unaccented lesson (performing the exercise in a specific location) causes a canine to wonder what he did wrong. The trainer said, "Sit," the dog sat and then just when pooch thought he'd done well and perhaps looked for some praise, he caught the dickens. That's sufficient to harden any animal. Overlooked is the obvious fact that insufficient attention must have been drawn to *where* the animal should sit. Otherwise, he'd comply. Canines seldom resist in halfway measure. (Recall chapter 1's mention of the absolute manner in which dogs perceive things: With them, it's either yes or no.) The pooch that sits on command will also do so where he senses he should, provided someone has shown him where that location is. If he sits but does so out of position, it's because he doesn't know the correct spot or—more likely—is unaware of its existence. A resistant dog won't sit at all.

Several manuals advocate the foregoing method. Many dictate that following an overextended period of such "teaching," the dog should be severely corrected should he fail to sit when and where commanded. Were the method effective, there'd be little occasion for overblown corrections.

Experience says that force is an inescapable training element. The variables are degree and frequency, which depend on one's reading of the dog. To use force techniques reasonably, *do so from day one*. Don't inadvertently mislead—be honest with the animal. He'll be corrected far less in the long run.

So what am I suggesting? That you teach the Sit by knocking your pet into position? Hardly. Read on.

The Sit—Preferred Teaching Method

The objective with this exercise is to teach it with minimal effort, simultaneously informing your pet that democracy is not a component of commands. To attain both goals, follow a simple procedure that capitalizes on natural canine tendencies instead of trying to defeat them.

First, reposition the pinch collar so that the chain portion is below the chin. Then maneuver the dog into such a position that—while he may not be looking directly at you—he's faced your way. This is accomplished merely by walking backward (a motion most canines follow) while not allowing pooch to drag you in another direction. Pat your leg to attract attention. Once your pal is in position—standing, facing generally toward you—command, "Sit" and immediately afterward, quickly leash-pull the dog so close to your front that he nearly touches you. Notice, I said *pull: Do not jerk the leash.* As you pull, keep your hands together and close to your body, at a level higher than the dog's head. The whole procedure should take about a second. Relax the leash pressure the instant your pet sits and praise, "Good Sit, Good Sit." Don't say anything other than that. By now your companion is likely realizing you're trying to communicate, and extra words make it that much harder for him to pick out the ones you want him to key on.

You'll discover that this move requires surprisingly little force, far less than the push-pull method necessitates. The illusion is that you're trying to pull the dog onto yourself. The reality is that nearly any canine thus pressured will reflexively dig in his back feet to compensate for the sudden shift in balance. That is, when one leash-pulls a dog in a given direction, the animal reacts by pulling in the opposite direction. This causes him to sit. The result is instant success for you both.

Accent your approval by stroking under the jaw, the idea being to teach pooch to look at you as he sits. Should he turn away, instantly stop petting. One doesn't reward for diverted attention, which continued caressing would do. As he looks back, resume petting. If you're working a small animal, you may have to kneel on one or both knees to accomplish this manner of praise, but you'll find the results worth the effort.

Keep the dog sitting for a brief interval to suggest that "Sit!" doesn't mean he should smack the ground with his derrière, only to run off seconds later. Petting usually keeps a dog in place, but don't hesitate to apply leash pressure, if need be. Again, relax the lead the moment pooch settles and begin petting once more. After a few moments, walk him a short distance, using encouragement like "C'mon, pup." Once you again have him in the proper facing position, repeat the procedure.

By the fourth demonstration, most respond correctly before leash pressure can be transmitted. If pooch is still uncertain what's expected, continue to demonstrate until he understands. Don't assume your friend is stupid if he is slow to catch on. Stress can inhibit learning. He's probably just nervous from these new goings-on. If he appears to comprehend intent but is trying to resist, apply pressure quicker and more forcefully. Also, allow a half second's response time after commanding "Sit," before applying force. Any animal needs reaction time, and pressure applied simultaneous with a command teaches that no matter how quickly the dog responds, he'll receive force anyway. (i.e., the lesson can become "Don't try to perform correctly, as I'll pressure you regardless.")

The first time your pet sits on command without help, praise that animal, "Good Sit, Good Sit." Share your pleasure. Smile, radiating enjoyment of the moment. It's a contagious attitude. While you're at it, give yourself some silent applause—you just communicated with another species.

Baseless Worries

Lest one conclude that this approach constitutes strangling a dog into position, put such concerns to rest. As stated in chapter 6, "Basic

The first step in teaching Sit—position the dog so he is looking toward you.

The second step in teaching the Sit. Upwardly directed leash pressure causes nearly any canine to sit. Note that the degree of force needed is minimal, even with this adult German Shepherd Dog.

Don't forget the all-important praise "Good Sit."

There're all kinds of "Sits" and varying manners of praise. During a first training session this kind of exchange is more than acceptable.

Tools," I use pinch collars. Unlike chokes, pinch collars don't strangle. They create pressure to the extent that force is transmitted through the leash. Owing to the direction of pull, most of the pressure occurs at the back of the neck. Because the collar's upper chain (to which the lead is attached) has been positioned at the front, it's located opposite the point of force and is thus pulled away from the windpipe. The lower chain contacts the front of the neck, true, but not with sufficient tension to cause even mild choking.

Second, only minimal force is needed to teach the Sit in this manner, usually *a good deal less* than the push-pull method takes. Little more than finger pressure is normally called for, even with large animals. Bear in mind, too, that teaching Sit via the push-pull process with a choke *does* strangle.

Third, if the technique throttled, not only would I neither employ it nor recommend it to you; it wouldn't work. If you've ever seen a dog at leash's end with his wind cut off, you know that he panics, often bucking away from the pressure's source. He may throw one or both front legs over the leash in attempt to reduce its tension. He certainly doesn't respond to command, not when his very survival seems threatened.

What I'm telling you is that this method is simple, easy, direct and honest. It has the built-in advantage of saying to your pet at the onset that commands aren't open to discussion; that he must comply. Furthermore, pooch learns to sit with such speed that when you advance to heeling— the next lesson—response to the Sit command is often so fast that a straight Sit at Heel results as a by-product.

I don't imply that every dog can be taught the commanded Sit using this approach. No method works with every pooch for every lesson. But of the thousands of dogs with whom I've had training experience, only a small fraction had to be shown the exercise via a different technique.

Temperament Problems

There are two groups of canines to whom teaching the Sit (or any lesson) by any means is difficult: the fighters and the highly insecure, ultrasubmissive individuals. Make no mistake, reference is made to *extreme* personalities, those found at opposite ends of the temperamental spectrum; not those only slightly tough or marginally tender. The fighter immediately and convincingly attacks anyone who tries to dominate him. The overly submissive dog responds to the slightest pressure by seeming to want to lie down and die.

Owners of dogs at either end of the continuum are encouraged to reread chapter 2, "The Right Dog." Should the problem be chronic, seek professional help. The former probably has murder in his heart; the latter, no heart at all. Both are probably genetically deficient. It's equally probable that neither can ever make a sound companion. If those strike you as harsh statements, they're also not easy to write. My purpose is to prevent pain and disappointment down the road. Formal training can't change any dog's essence. Nothing alters maladaptive genetics or profound and prolonged environmental influences. An effective program enhances what's already there, but it creates nothing.

What Have You Said?

Before continuing, ponder the events of the past few minutes. What have you actually taught your pet? Obviously you've shown what Sit means, but is that all? Not by a long shot.

You've implied the meaning of "Good" by associating the word with physical praise. You've demonstrated that you're in charge and that your words are to be obeyed. You've said to your pet that you have things to say to him, things to teach. You've gotten his attention; you've started to build a bridge. Rarely does any one lesson contain but a single motive.

A Seldom-Mentioned Point

Keep in mind that sitting isn't the most natural stationary position for a dog. When you observe canines at rest, notice that most are either lying down or standing. Few will be sitting. The posture is a transitory position. Dogs generally use it when changing from standing to lying down and vice versa.

Thus, if an animal being taught Sit initially attempts to stand or lie down in response, don't assume that you're seeing disobedience per se. Your pet could be interpreting "Sit" as "Rest," and it's foolish to admonish a canine that is trying his level best to please or is simply reacting like a dog. If he breaks from the Sit, put him back into position, but use no more force than necessary. Should he lie down, leash-pull or collar-lift him into the sitting posture. Don't yank upward on the lead— that's too harsh at this stage—pull it.

ON-LEASH HEELING

Heeling Defined

Rather than merely commanding, "Take a walk with me," the heeling command directs a dog to maintain a constant position relative to the handler's left side. As a particularly apt student once observed, "In a sense, heeling connotes a moving stay just left of the trainer."

When to Commence Teaching

You may be able to proceed with this work after only three or four Sit demonstrations, or you may have to wait a few days until pooch internalizes the Sit. Only you can make that judgment. My advice is, if your pet's attention has been riveted on you since the first Sit presentation and if he comprehends the lesson, continue into heeling instruction during this initial session. If the two of you are on a roll, stay with it. On the other hand, should either of you be experiencing difficulty or if you're unsure whether to proceed now, observe the adage "When in doubt, don't." There's no rush.

"On My Left Side? But I'm Right-handed."

Many a novice has made that observation when discovering that our number-one friend traditionally heels at the left side. Granted, to a person just getting started in obedience, the positioning can seem awkward (especially to a right-handed individual). However, the answer to "How come?" is contained in the above subheading. Since most are right-handed, having the dog to the left leaves one's good hand free for delicate work, such as unlocking a door (try it with your off-hand sometime), shaking hands with someone or carrying a package.

Origination of Left-Side Heeling

A consensus among many professionals is that much of what is customary canine-handling practice today has grown out of safe handling of dogs around firearms. Like the majority of people, most cops, soldiers and hunters are right-handed. Having the dog on the left leaves the strong hand free for holding or using a gun or for other purposes. A dog on the left is reckoned at a safe distance from any firearm being carried. Also, while the practice is more result than cause, heeling on the left is mandatory should one show in obedience competition.

However, there's no law against right-side heeling. If that's your preference, just hold a mental mirror to the instructions about heeling and related work.

Leash Position Versus Size of Dog

The correct leash position for teaching heeling is the one that works best for you. My preference for medium to large dogs has the leash in the right hand, about waist high, with sufficient slack to hang just below the left knee. With smaller breeds the lead is easier to handle left-handed, leaving the right free for praising. Should either position seem clumsy, modify the technique to one more suitable. You've enough to deal with right now without having to worry about managing your lead according to someone else's notion of how it should be done.

Lest you fall into the trap of guiding your dog, however, keep your hands near or below waist level. Moreover, avoid extending the leash arm above your head. Such an awkward position not only hampers control; it can appear threatening to the dog to the extent that it can cause lagging.

Teaching On-Leash Heeling

Reposition the pinch collar so that the chain portion is at the back of the neck. Check that pooch's ears aren't pinned by the links. You're ready to begin.

Start by commanding, "Sit," to commence from a position of control. Locate yourself squarely at your pet's right side, his shoulder adjacent to your left leg. This is the Heel position. Endeavor to establish at least momentary eye contact by gentle petting, saying your pal's name and use of body language (such as slightly tilting your head and shoulders to the right). Once you have pooch's best attention, command, "Fuss," and walk to a nearby, predetermined spot.

Understandably, a dog couldn't know much about Fuss at this stage. The animal may be aware you're trying to tell him something, but it's doubtful that any canine can deduce the concept of heeling in a few seconds. He may trot along with you; he may not. Patting your leg coincident with command can help get him moving. Regardless of response, however—even if he shoots away in pursuit of things interesting to canines—don't respond with a turn-him-inside-out, leash-yank correction. Once Fuss's meaning is clear, you can and should lower the boom should he flee, but not yet. For now, return to the techniques outlined under the section "Leash Taming" (i.e., quickly walk in the direction away from the one your dog took), the only new element being to gradually let out less and less slack, causing the pinch collar to bite quicker in relation to the animal's "See you later!"

Mechanics

Start on your left foot during these first heeling lessons. Its being nearer to the dog facilitates keying on the movement. The technique makes it easier for pooch to start with you instead of a beat late. Of equal importance is stopping on your right foot: As you halt, don't swing your left foot past your right to take another step. A proper stop teaches a smooth, glide sit, since the procedure makes it easier for the dog to discern that you are indeed stopping. He sees that the leg closer to him has halted, and he follows suit.

For Future Reference

Lest you think that you'll have to walk in contrived fashion for the rest of your days, be aware that these patterns are used to facilitate canine learning. Once the meaning of Fuss is clear, it makes no difference which foot you start or stop on. In point of fact, once my dogs are comfortable with these first training stages, I habitually initiate movement with the right foot, especially with competition animals. The practice has several advantages, not the least of which is causing pooch to be more attentive to command. It also creates a "heeling pocket" and lessens the chance of blocking psychic contact by bumping the dog with my first step. I want my pet close (but not touching), and I don't wish to risk stifling attraction by brushing aside an attentive muzzle as we begin walking. A novice animal could mistakenly interpret being bumped away as rejection.

To Continue with Heeling

As your dog takes his very first step with you, praise "Good Fuss, Good Fuss!" Do this just as soon as he moves, but keep walking—don't stop to praise. Approval at that instant communicates far better than praise given while merely walking along in a straight line. When he responds to Fuss by coming out of the Sit or when he alters course in response to your direction change, pooch is more aware of keying on your actions than when just jogging along at your side. Much value is derived from timing praise coincident with a dog's initiation of effort.

As you stop, command, "Sit," and immediately cause your pal to

The enforced Sit in the Heel position. Note the trainer's constant attention on his charge and the method of praising *under* the dog's muzzle.

108

sit in the Heel position. Turning your upper body toward him as you direct Sit can facilitate the correct response. (Your action imparts a measure of controlling, body-language pressure.) Keep attention on you during this interlude by gentle under-chin petting while praising, ''Good Sit.'' Don't permit the dog to respond to petting by breaking from position. Demonstrate early on that he's not to move until you command, ''Fuss.''

Don't harshly correct if the animal sits crookedly. Likely he's doing so merely to keep an eye on you. Rather than condemn initiative, deflect the problem by heeling closely to the right of fences, buildings and similar structures. The method affords pooch a gentle opportunity to develop the desired habit, since there's no space left to sit askew.

Is He Being Disobedient or Being a Dog?

A canine that resists directives must be dealt with to the degree that he finds it is in his interests to get with the program. However, a trainer must be careful not to misinterpret confusion as contention, responding with correction instead of further communication.

When first teaching heeling, don't harshly correct if the dog forges ahead. The canine tendency to blaze the way is as natural as rain. A tough correction at this juncture could communicate that *he* dissatisfies you, that there's something wrong with him as a dog. Essentially, it would give a dog the devil for being a dog. Pull back on the lead and tell the animal, ''No—(*pause*)—Fuss,'' patting your leg to aid understanding. Corrections for forging are proper after heeling is understood, but not until then.

Heeling Technique

Move fast and with purpose. Aimlessly shuffling along bores a dog, especially during early stages of teaching heeling. Moving quickly requires fixating attention on you. It causes having to *work* at staying with you, which is the whole idea. If you try to make heeling easy, your pal can lose interest for want of stimulation.

Keep your eyes on pooch and his attention on you. Much of what you should be teaching him is to use his powers of concentration. This doesn't mean the animal has to keep his eyes riveted on you during heeling. That makes for nervous walking (try it yourself: walking without looking where you're going) and smacks of enslavement, which is hardly the goal. The animal has to keep track of your whereabouts; how he does that is his business. Accordingly, should pooch drift to the left, turn right. If he shoots ahead of you, immediately reverse course.

As much as possible, perform only straight-line heeling during this first session. Make no turns except to correct or to keep from walking out of the training area. Second, introduce heeling with short walks between each Sit. Since commands occur less often, uninterrupted, prolonged heeling at this stage only affords opportunity for distraction. Besides, the quicker you walk and the more often you stop, the sooner your companion will learn Automatic Sit (See p. 111). Heeling can get only so good in one session, but the odds are excellent that the Auto-Sit concept can be learned in moments. This is especially true if you command, "Fusssit," stringing out the "S" sound while taking only one or two heeling steps between Sits. The message, of course, is that Fuss leads to Sit.

A Sometimes Problem

Confusion causes some dogs to balk during initial heeling instruction. The problem can be overcome merely by facing the animal and taking your first steps backward. Nearly any dog will follow this inviting motion. Turn back into normal walking mode as pooch begins to trot along. Another deflective technique has the handler commanding, "Fuss," stepping forward a pace, turning left to cross in front of the stationary student, then turning left again 90 degrees and walking past the animal's left side. The suggestive motion of the trainer's passing legs often entices even a stubborn canine to join the parade.

"I Will Not!"

A small percentage of hard-core "refuseniks" exist. They resist attempts to be led regardless of inducements. With one of this minority, whose aspect suggests neither fear nor confusion but an air of "No, I won't go with you," first enlist a family member or close friend to work the dog. Bad chemistry *can* exist. If this is unsuccessful, reclaim the leash and start the dog again. Failing any attitudinal improvement after trying the techniques described in the preceding subsection, turn your back on the dog and commence walking as though he weren't at leash's end. That is, if you're convinced that confusion or anxiety isn't the obstacle, that you're being challenged by so obstinate a dog that he allows himself to literally be dragged on his back, so be it.

This remedy isn't enjoyable, and it should be resorted to only after all other approaches have been exhausted. Go this route if you must, however; extended coaxing and cajoling at this stage merely solidify a stubborn canine's resolve. (Oddly, after realizing they've met their match in stubbornness, such animals often make outstanding obedience performers.)

Loose Leash

When teaching heeling, beginning trainers sometimes try to hang on to an illusion of control and a feeling of security by maintaining a taut leash rather than keeping it somewhat slack, as it should be. The result is guiding or attempting to guide the dog. Don't do it.

Though it may feel foreign at first, keep a slack leash during heeling, for three major reasons. First, through a tight lead the dog can feel where the trainer is: The animal doesn't have to work at heeling and thus never learns that maintaining the Heel position is his responsibility. Pooch is taught that it's the trainer's job to keep him in the proper position. Secondly, a tight leash transmits continual pinch-collar pressure, with the result that the dog is being corrected with every step he takes, *even though he may be trying to do the right thing.* Last, a tight lead can cause a dog to pull away from the source of the pressure, which results in heeling wide. As mentioned in the section that deals with teaching the Sit, ". . . when one leash-pulls a dog in a given direction, the animal reacts by pulling in the opposite direction."

AUTOMATIC SIT

Perspective

Precision heeling is one of the more difficult exercises for a dog to master, if for no other reason than so many facets are attendant to the work. During heeling, a dog can lag behind, forge ahead, swing wide or crowd the handler. With Automatic Sit, however, less can go wrong: The animal either sits or doesn't. If he does, the Sit is either performed in the Heel position or isn't. Hence, focus on getting the good Sit when starting a novice. Bear with that neophyte's heeling efforts. Don't try to perfect them in an afternoon.

Purpose

More than one beginning trainer has asked about Automatic Sit's purpose—why it's taught. Though a common answer is that it's a competition standard, its real-world function is to provide control. Without this requirement, or one like it (such as Automatic Stand in Place), additional commands would be needed to keep your dog next to you when meeting an acquaintance during a walk, for instance. Otherwise, pooch would be wrapping the leash around the person's legs, determining gender and generally being a nuisance.

Teaching

You've been telling pooch "Sit" each time you stop walking. To extend this behavior into an automatic function, merely phase out the verbal command by gradually softening your voice, replacing it with increasing collar pressure as you stop moving.

Clarity

Once pooch sits automatically as you stop walking, drop the verbal Sit command altogether. Why? Because it's obvious that he's taking your cessation of motion as a cue to sit. If you were to continue commanding "Sit," the animal could reasonably assume that he's missed the point of the lesson, that since you'll always command "Sit," he needn't sit automatically.

An Important Juncture

The first time your dog sits automatically marks a critical moment. You must acknowledge the event to reinforce that the Auto-Sit is what you've been trying to teach. Look at your pet for a second, radiating pleasant surprise—"Well, now! Look at you!"—accenting that you've indeed seen what he's done, and communicate warm, sincere approval.

Responsibility

As mentioned earlier, once a dog appears to understand any command's meaning, he becomes responsible for it. From the occasion of pooch's first Auto-Sit, correct anytime he fails to sit automatically. Continue with Good Sit praise for a few days, however. You'll be using the Sit cue later with other lessons, and even quick learners must hear a word several times to lock the sound into their minds.

Another method of enforcing the Automatic Sit. This technique requires good balance and a light touch. The startle effect is the governing factor here, not raw force. Properly done, the dog won't be able to understand how you touched him, just that you did. Note that contact is made with the handler's instep, not with the toe.

Ineffective Correction Styles

Automatic Sit leash corrections are sometimes depicted as jerking the lead in straight-up (or slightly forward and upward) fashion. That style is proper only occasionally. Often the method teaches a rock-back Sit: The dog stops and steps backward a pace before sitting, thereby placing himself out of position behind the trainer. With very large dogs and dogs with very strong neck muscles, many handlers (especially beginners) find it nearly impossible to effect an adequate correction using the straight-up technique. Sufficient leverage can't be achieved from an angle directly over the dog's head, although considerable force can be effected through the semi-right-angle correction described below.

Effective Correction Styles

Correct for failing to sit automatically by tugging the lead upward and in the direction of your right shoulder. Don't merely pull—yank and release: Don't keep applying pressure after the animal has sat. As always, the degree of force must befit your pet's size, touch sensitivity (or lack) and temperament.

With tall, body-sensitive dogs, one can correct adequately using a southpaw, open-handed finger swat to the rear, just above the tail. Make the move quickly, returning the hand to your side as part of the swatting motion. The key is the startle effect, as opposed to pure pressure, leaving the dog asking, "How'd you do that?" (The answer, of course, is "Don't worry how I did it; you just Sit.") Know that this correction can be applied only two or three times during an entire training program: More frequent use leads a canine to look backward as he sits.

A Final Thought About Sitting

Once in a while a dog that has learned both Sit on command and Automatic Sit at Heel does an amusing thing: He sits whenever he nears the trainer. You're reading the paper, your pet wanders over and sits. You're taking off your coat, pooch trots up and sits. You're stretched out on the couch, and here comes your pal, sitting upon arrival. In each case, the animal looks at you expectantly after plunking down his bottom. He's seeking approval, and you should respond with warm, sincere praise. True, you didn't command "Sit," and while technicians might claim that the behavior constitutes anticipation (executing a command before it's given), you should be counting your blessings. You have a friend that is trying to please you. That's a gift.

SIT-STAY

Introduce this exercise between the second and fifth working session, depending on how your pet is handling the lessons so far.

Deal from Confidence

To instill security in a dog's mind, initial Stays are best practiced near buildings, fences and the like. This is not to suggest leaving pooch propped against an old storage shed, but near such a structure. Were first Stays taught in large, open areas, anxiety could accompany the lessons. In such settings a dog can feel exposed and threatened: "They (whatever *they* might be) can come at me from anywhere!" Learned nervousness— often manifested by rapid panting and darting glances—is difficult to eradicate.

Teaching the Sit-Stay

Start with your pet sitting at Heel. The leash should have very little slack and be held in your left hand. Simultaneously give the Stay signal— holding the right palm a few inches in front of the animal's nose— command "Stay," and step away one long pace. As a continuation of this movement, turn and face your pal, continuing to hold your palm toward him. After five seconds, pivot back to the Heel position and praise, "Good Stay" while petting under the chin.

Praise calmly, not making the approval so effusive that it excites pooch into moving from position. Also, praise only *after* you've rearrived in the Heel position. Praising from afar can trigger movement leading to an improper, set-up correction.

Gradually increase time and distance over the next few sessions, the week's objective being six feet for one minute.

I Know You Heard Me, But . . .

That last phrase needs emphasizing: *Gradually increase*. I'll grant you, stays can be boring, for trainer and trainee alike. There's a tendency

Teaching the Sit-Stay.

to counter the monotony by rushing ahead to greater distances and longer times prematurely. However, it's essential to lengthen both almost imperceptibly. I speechify to first-week students as follows:

> Don't tell me next week your dog will hold a twenty-foot Stay. Six feet is the present limit, and for good reason. Should your pet move when you're several yards distant, by the time you can return to correct, the optimum moment for teaching has passed.

The time to correct for a broken Stay is when the animal is one blink into movement, when his aspect reveals he's just on the verge of breaking. Minimal force—often a leash flick or verbal warning—is required at that instant, but this can't be accomplished when the handler is several paces removed. Take your time. You can always move farther away.

Stay Procedures

To avoid confusion, habitually leave on your right foot. Its movement is less likely to pull your pet along, for it's farther from him. In terms of body language, leaving on the left foot obstructs your aura of control from a dog's perspective. It creates a fleeting wall. Lastly, avoid staring at your charge as you depart, lest your eyes pull him along. Keep track of pooch peripherally. There's less chance he'll misunderstand and follow. (The practice also enables you to respond faster should he break: Human peripheral vision detects movement quicker than does direct viewing.)

Once your pet is reliable for twenty seconds, rather than remain in place and stare at the animal, move around. This often leads a dog to develop the habit of keeping his eyes on the owner during a Stay (a desirable end in itself), if for no other reason than to see what the person is up to. Pooch may turn his head to watch as you walk about, but he may not move from position. (I teach my dogs that they may not move a front paw during a Stay.) The only functional setting in which one would leave his or her dog, go a short distance, turn and face the animal for an extended period while remaining stationary is in competition. Teach useful Stays by practicing in realistic contexts. After leaving pooch, walk around as though searching for a dropped article, open and shut a gate, tie a shoe, move some lawn furniture and so forth. Make it appear you left for a reason.

After returning to the Heel position, don't permit any departure from the Sit until you command, "Fuss." As stated earlier, should the animal stir during praise, impede movement instantly, then continue your approval. A dog must be made to see that praise doesn't signify release from command.

Stay Corrections

Should a dog who understands Stay move from position, the rule is to immediately respond with "No" and to leash-correct him back to where he was. This isn't done by mere guiding. The dog is forcefully returned to where he was left. Accompany this action with an oration akin to "I told you to Stay! When I tell you to Stay, by heaven you Stay!" The purpose of such sermonizing is to make the lesson abundantly clear. The words themselves mean nothing, of course, but the tone and repetitious use of Stay conveys intent, and it helps put you in the proper frame of mind.

Verbal Bridge

This is an important notion with regard to broken Stays. If the dog moves from an assigned position, your immediate response should be "No!" (which translates as "Never!") The purpose is to pinpoint for your friend exactly where in time he went wrong. Otherwise, if you're several steps removed, by the time you can correct pooch, the meaning may be unclear. The animal could think that the mistake he made was the direction he took or the speed at which he took it. This verbal-association technique will prove essential as distance increases.

It Can Be Confusing

The concept of a command that directs inaction can perplex a canine. He effects motion in response to Sit, and he moves when hearing Fuss. When first told "Stay," the reaction can be "How's that? Do what?" Since earlier commands have instructed him to do something, pooch may reasonably expect that any command calls for action on his part. Hence, confusion can arise when he's first shown that Stay directs, "Do nothing." When leaving your dog for the first time, be ready to instantly flick the leash backward at the first hint of movement. You'll not only need less force; you'll prevent trouble down the road.

It's a Double

Stay is actually a double or second command. If a dog is told "Sit," then there's an end of it. Sit doesn't mean that a canine should smack the ground with his butt, only to run off seconds later. Following Sit with Stay tells the animal to keep sitting, which he should do until the next command, anyway. The only reason for teaching Stay is that more *people* are more comfortable with the concept than without it.

"What if Pooch Lies Down?"

Should your sitting dog lie down during a Stay, immediately erupt with "No" and leash-lift him into the Sit position. Then leave again for a short time, affording the opportunity to successfully complete the Stay.

Correct for the Right Reason

Should pooch bark at something during a Stay, correct him for breaking the Stay—even if he held the commanded position—not for the specific reason he had in barking. The message is that part of Stay is to remain quiet. The correction is an open-handed reminder (tailored to the dog's sensitivity—a finger tap may be adequate) under the muzzle, accompanied by "No—I said, 'Stay.' " Yes, this constitutes repeating a command, but the communication is needed, or the animal may have difficulty understanding intent.

A BEGINNING- AND END-OF-SESSION OBEDIENCE FUNCTION

Starting a couple of days after the first session, teach your pet he must sit before the collar will be put on and that he's not going anywhere without it. At my kennels the dog that rebels against this dictum finds himself left in his run and treated to watching other dogs while they're being worked, each having a grand time of it. When next told to sit for the collar, one can often hear the dog's derriere hit the ground. At that point, genuine communication is occurring.

I'm told this technique might make a dog jealous. Jealousy is a human emotion, not belonging to the canine world. Projecting human traits to lower animals is an uninformed practice at best, an irrational one at worst. All a dog knows when he sees other animals involved in activity is that he is not so involved. His way of perceiving this is on the order of "the I and the Not-I," "I" being the canine in question; "the Not-I," any other creature.

Theory aside, one shouldn't have to put up with foolishness in order to spend time with his or her best friend. Demanding the Sit while attaching (or removing) the collar also subtly initiates the concept of off-leash (and off-collar) obedience: The dog is learning to be responsible for his behavior *even before the collar is on.* He's learning to respond to you, not just to equipment. The animal is also learning to be responsive at a place other than the training area. A dog can learn his lessons, but as long as he performs them only in one location, he won't necessarily be obedient elsewhere. This procedure subtly initiates the process of adapting training to the real world.

Reflection

If the old dog bark, he gives counsel.

George Herbert, Jacula Prudentum

9

Second Week

HEEL ON LEASH AND AUTOMATIC SIT

Adjustments

At this time, begin to incorporate turns and variations in pace during heeling. As your pet learns to handle abrupt changes in direction and speed, time your "Good Fuss" praise with his effort: *as* he fights to stay with you on a turn, for instance. If pooch's height is conducive to the action, accompany the approval with under-chin petting while moving at heel. Yes, it's something of a contortion to praise in this manner, but try it and watch the reaction before deciding if it's worth the effort. You'll have a prancer on your hands, literally.

Turns

As one might suppose, there are three turns: Left, right and about. Make them precisely: rights and lefts at 90 degrees, abouts at 180 degrees. Don't merely saunter into a turn—make it sharply. That's far more instructive and effective in maintaining attention.

Immediately flick the leash if your pal loses concentration during a right or an about-turn. Accompany this action with a verbal admonition

Schutzhund-style about-turns. The handler has turned 180 degrees to his left, causing the Airedale to circle behind him.

of "No!—(*pause*)—Fuss!" Knee pooch from your path if he gets in your way during a left turn, targeting the neck rather than the head or shoulder and adding the same spoken censure. (Use the area just above your kneecap, not the kneecap itself.) Be aware that applying the knee-bump correction to a hot-tempered dog can trigger an aggressive response. With a tiny animal, use the side of your instep to nudge him from your path.

No, I'm not suggesting you kick your pet. Perish the thought. The idea isn't to scare or injure. When correctly applied, the correction has more the effect of forcefully brushing the animal aside, mindful of body mass and temperament. What you're saying is "Look, dog, I'll make you a deal: You work at staying out of my path, and I won't have to knock you out of the way." You're reaffirming that it's *his* responsibility to keep track of you, not the other way around.

Important: When disciplining your companion for blowing any turn, follow the correction by repeating the maneuver a few times successively to provide immediate opportunities for successful negotiation. When he handles the move correctly, praise "Good Fuss, Good Fuss," *as he does so*. Make it obvious you're proud of him for doing well.

Initially practice about-turns by pivoting to the right, not to the left. The method is easier for a canine to follow. Incidentally, in AKC obedience trials, about-turns must be made in this manner. As proficiency grows, effect about-turns by spinning 180 degrees toward the left, causing pooch to have to circle behind you into the Heel position. Pass the leash behind your back in the process. This style of about-turn is required in Schutzhund competition. If a correction is required, effect it immediately after the turn by jerking the leash forward while it's still in your right hand. Delaying the pressure until the lead has been passed behind your back is too long after the infraction to be productive.

Changes in Speed

Be obvious when changing speed. When implementing a slow step, for instance, make it on the order of a stalking pace, which is helpful in capturing focus. Its contrast to normal walking draws attention to the moment. When you speed up, don't merely shuffle along: Sprint. Be careful with the quicker pace—rapid motion tends to excite, and an inexperienced animal can bump you or get underfoot such that you lose your balance.

To cure the slow start. This Doberman Pinscher has decided there's a camera to be stared at and that she'll Fuss when she gets around to it. A split second after this photograph was taken, the force of the leg correction—tempered to her size and toughness—brought her to the situation.

124

Challenge Your Dog

The subtitle's message isn't that one should give a dog more than he can handle. Anyone can lose a novice animal on a sudden turn, but such deceit is not only unfair; it simply isn't the idea. Challenge a dog according to his level of understanding and ability—that's the idea! Make heeling just difficult enough that he has to work at it. Interest can wane should one attempt to make a canine's job easy. The dog finds no meat in the work to stimulate him. Pack heritage has preconditioned pooch to not only accept teamwork but to thrive on it.

Slow Starts and Lagging

If your companion is developing the habit of starting late or lagging behind, rectify the problem before it becomes ingrained. With pooch in the Heel position, hold the leash right-handed at waist level, with slack hanging slightly below your left knee. With your feet together, allow yourself to tip forward. Just before the moment when you must take a step to preserve verticality, command "Fuss," and shoot your left leg forward. The leg will strike the leash with considerable force. If your pet starts forward coincident with command, he'll be in proper position and will receive no correction. Should he lag, however, one or two applications of the technique will cure the laxity. Know that timing is critical in this procedure. Command "Fuss," *just prior* to (not coincident with) taking your first step. Even the fastest worker needs reaction time. The force of your leg striking the leash is part of what teaches the dog to start quickly. The other element is that the method also causes you to start briskly, a contagious attitude.

Should your pet start properly but lag once you're moving, position the leash as described, causing your left leg to strike it as a by-product of walking. If pooch maintains the Heel position, he'll receive no correction. If he drops behind, the technique will bring him along quickly.

Be aware that the foregoing practices are not intended for small dogs. Were either procedure used with a Toy Poodle, for instance, the force of the leg hitting the lead could toss the dog into the next county. For smaller animals, a sharp left-handed motion into the leash immediately after "Fuss" serves the same purpose but applies less force.

The Trailer

Another laggard is the dog that travels not merely a pace or two behind the handler but directly behind the ankles. Herding dogs often do this. Correct the problem by quickly turning left a full 180 degrees the instant your pet darts behind you. This causes the animal to find himself in the Heel position—at your left side—but facing the wrong direction. The angle allows application of a forceful correction using minimal effort.

"But I Itch, You See"

A seemingly less intentioned type of lagging occurs when a dog decides it's time to stop for a quick scratch. Keep walking. Demonstrate that your commands transcend momentary needs. Pooch can scratch on his own time. Besides, if the dog learns he can stop you either by scratching, stretching, shaking, yawning or by any other ruse, then the question becomes one of whom is heeling whom?

The Call of Nature

"But what if he stops to relieve himself?" That, too, he can learn to take care of during his off hours. Keep moving. If you ever *need* to move your dog hurriedly from point "A" to point "B," you won't want to wait for him to first make a deposit.

Forging Ahead

To correct the forger, merely stop walking. The animal will blow the Automatic Sit because he'll be out of position: He'll be ahead of you. As you stop, immediately leash-yank the critter to a point a foot or so behind you. Then tug him forward into the Heel position. This generally cures forging in short order.

To the dog that decides he can manipulate the situation by hurriedly backing into position as you stop, wish him "Lots of luck!" He'll discover that your alertness led to starting the correction before he could even begin to scoot back.

"You Stand on it; May I?"

A stunt to which some canines are disposed while sitting at Heel is placing the right front paw on the handler's left foot. While one trainer might say that this has to do with the animal asserting dominance, another might use the term "passive resistance." My thought is that the animal is contacting the handler for reasons ranging from insecurity to affection. Most likely he's simply keeping track of you.

In any case, it's a trivial matter that's easily cured by lightly pressing your right foot against the errant paw's right side. Massive compression is neither necessary nor desirable—there's no need to risk spraining or breaking toes. This is a good example of the principle that says corrections aren't so much a matter of "How hard?" as "How quickly?"

The Tower of Pisa Syndrome

Similar to the "Whither thou goest" attitude portrayed above is the pooch that is right at home leaning against the trainer's leg. It's an annoyance, but one that's sometimes better temporarily endured than reflexively corrected. If your companion has this tendency, defer correction until you're convinced he won't interpret your reaction—bumping him away either with the side of your left knee or foot, depending on his size—as rejection. Leaning by a very young dog, or one that is unaccustomed to being around other animals and suddenly finds himself in a first-week obedience class, for instance, should be tolerated until some measure of confidence is seen. Premature corrective action could cloud the intended messages—merely wanting your own space and that pooch doesn't need you (or anyone else) to prop him up, physically or emotionally. Don't risk telling an immature or nervous dog that he's not wanted or that his contact offends.

Once correction is appropriate, should obstinacy come into play— whereby a knee bump elicits glaring and pressing harder—the situation has changed and so should your response. One or two healthy collar blasts leftward, accompanied by "No!—(*pause*)—Sit!" (Sit also means "without leaning against me") usually constitute sufficient rehabilitation. Thoroughness calls for a quick Fuss for a few steps and praise of Good Sit as the dog shows you by sitting without leaning that he understands.

Crowding

The leaner's cousin is the crowder: The dog that insists on riding against your leg during heeling. The cure for a touch-sensitive animal may be carrying the leash left-handed so that it hangs between your leg and the dog. An impressionable canine is averse to brushing against a lead. If this has no effect, correct with a series of bumps to the neck area with your left knee as you walk, coupled as needed with outward leash yanks. Complement either action with "No!—Fuss!" As the dog begins to walk properly, show approval with "Good Fuss," lest he mistakenly infer that you don't want any contact with him.

Heeling Wide

Antithetical to the crowder is the canine that heels appreciably to the left. If you suspect that your pet's wide heeling is a product of fear rather than disobedience, as can be the case with a new animal that has a history of abuse, spoken and gestured encouragement is the best route. If the problem has its roots in stubbornness, a series of right turns often brings such a dog into line. If that proves insufficient, use right-handed leash pops toward yourself, adding the verbal admonition "No!—Fuss!" as you continue walking. In any case, be sure to praise "Good Fuss" as the dog properly aligns himself.

Crooked Sits

A common heeling problem is the crooked Sit. By crooked I'm not referring to a Sit that's off-line by a sixteenth of an inch, so to speak. I don't call Sits that closely, and I suggest you shouldn't, either.

Every trainer has his or her own definition of the line between an acceptably straight Sit and one that isn't. My rule is that if my dog heels in position, sits squarely and in rhythm as I stop and doesn't push himself out from or lean against me, I'm satisfied.

The unaligned Sit that can lead to real problems is characterized by the dog sitting perpendicular to the handler. Unless you're a competition devotee, even this degree of sitting askew isn't a serious problem in and of itself, but it can and usually does develop into more significant difficulties. The canine that sits that crookedly will generally extend the behavior to sitting in front of the handler. Eventually the animal won't sit at all.

A common correction in this situation is left-handed swatting or pulling the dog into position. This is mostly ineffective because for many canines the technique represents little more than rough petting—praise for doing the wrong thing!

Take one of two approaches to correct the problem, depending on its severity, duration and the dog's motivation, size and temperament. With an inexperienced animal, conduct a good deal of heeling adjacent to fences and such to your left, making other than straight sits impossible—no room is left for pooch to swing his rear away. Over time this practice normally instills the proper action.

With the canine that requires sterner reinforcement, yank him behind and slightly to your left, then jerk the animal forward into position. Now quickly heel two or three paces and halt to determine if the message got through. Praise sincerely if it did, but if repetitious force is needed, so be it. Keep in mind that this seldom-needed correction is intended only for dogs whose attitude isn't just "No!" but "Hell, no!" Sure, it's semirough treatment, but some canine's attitudes demand entry into their violent world. That's why it's reserved only for dogs that send the message "I know what you want, but I'll defy you, anyway." Such disrespect can never be tolerated.

"Sit Straight!"

A trap some trainers slide into is teaching "Sit Straight." The dog sits crookedly at heel, and the handler responds by taking a step or two forward, flicking the leash and commanding, "Sit Straight." Sure enough, pooch usually squares up somewhat.

However, a straight Sit is an Automatic-Sit requirement, not an afterthought. What's taking place is double commanding, since Fuss says—among other things—"Sit Straight." Responding to a crooked sit with other than instructive compulsion makes as much sense as not correcting for failure to Auto-Sit at Heel.

DOWN-STAY

Look Out!

Unlikely as it may be, if your dog is ever going to snap at you, he may do so while being shown the Down-Stay, regardless of instruction method. You're not only physically exposed, down is a very submissive posture, and some dominant canines won't accept their perceived lessening of status without rebellion.

Teaching the Platz—Medium to Large Dogs

Position the pinch collar with the chain portion along the front of the neck. With pooch sitting at heel, kneel alongside him and grasp the lead left-handed an inch or two from where it attaches to the collar.

This is a graphic depiction of how easily intent can be misunderstood when teaching the Platz from in front of a dog. Note the uncertainty as to what's wanted expressed by this Rottweiler's body language.

This alternate method of teaching Platz is especially handy when working with a particularly dominant animal, which this American Staffordshire Terrier is. Notice how the position protects the trainer's hand should a resentful bite be attempted.

Command, "Platz," and simultaneously pat the ground right-handed just in front of your pet. Apply suggestive downward leash pressure, tugging slightly toward yourself instead of in a straight-down direction. The purposes are to create an angle from which force can more easily be exerted and to avoid spraining a leg. Push the shoulders downward to aid communication. Praise, "Good Platz," as pooch reaches terra firma and instantly direct "Stay," momentarily reinforcing the command with the Stay hand signal.

Teaching the Platz—Small Dogs

With pooch sitting at heel, kneel on one or both knees alongside him. Place your left palm on his shoulders and your right hand just behind the front legs. Command, "Platz." A blink later, sweep the front legs forward while pushing downward on the shoulders. Praise "Good Platz" as the dog contacts the ground, and immediately command, "Stay" adding the Stay hand signal. Should leash pressure be needed to get or keep the animal on the ground, first position the pinch collar so that the chain portion is under the front of the neck.

Next to the Dog—Not in Front of Him

Positioning yourself in front of the dog when teaching Platz is a technical error. It can say to pooch that he should come to you prior to grounding or crawl to you just after. Of course, neither action is desirable. We're trying to teach your dog to go to ground and Stay. Remain next to him when teaching Platz.

Platz also Means "and Stay"

During the initial teaching session, command "Stay" with the same firmness of voice as "Platz." Tomorrow, soften the Stay command somewhat. Moderate the volume further the day after that. By the fourth session, you should be giving the Stay command in a stage whisper. By the fifth, it should have disappeared altogether. The idea is to build the concept of Stay into the Platz through association; to teach that Platz means "Hit the ground *and* remain in place." One may continue to use Stay if desired, but the idea behind this structuring is to eliminate the need.

An Alternative Teaching Method

Should pooch resist Platz overtures, enforce your will as follows. Starting with your pet in the Heel position, firmly grasp the upper left side of the neck left-handed and pull down toward your left leg, sliding your leg out of the way as needed. (Don't attempt to push straight down; some dogs will resist such force by bracing the front legs.) The dog will land on his right side instead of in a perfectly straight position, but keep in mind that the first objective is to get him on the ground. Settle for that for now, especially if there's been resistance. The position can be improved later, after pooch is grounding reliably. As your dog touches earth, praise "Good Platz," and command "Stay."

Teaching the Platz: Days Two, Three, Four etc.

The following day make one minor adjustment: Bend at the waist when commanding "Platz," rather than first kneeling on the ground. Gradually adjust your stance over the next few days, the goal being to direct Platz from a normal posture.

A Note About Praising

When petting in the Down position, do so under the chin or along the side of the head. Stroking a dog atop the head (or the back or shoulders) often induces pushing against the pleasant sensation to the extent that he attempts to rise. Later, one can and should use this subtle form of distraction conditioning, but not while teaching the new lesson.

No Heeling

After pooch has been grounded a short time, walk him a few feet and repeat the exercise. For now don't move him, using "Fuss." It's too soon to integrate Platz with other lessons. "Come on, pup," or some such, is preferable because if his heeling is off just then, you'd have to deal with that aspect when teaching a new command. Any necessitated heeling corrections could prejudice perception of either routine in terms of the other. Ergo, to avoid the possibility of heeling difficulties while teaching the new work, don't say "Fuss," in the first place.

A second reason for not coupling heeling with initial Platz lessons is the adverse effect that can result regarding Automatic Sit. If shown Platz several times in succession with heeling and Automatic Sit between each demonstration, a dog could conclude that Automatic Sit is being replaced by Automatic Platz. Remember, *Canis familiaris* is a behaviorally patterned animal.

To Make Life Easier

Simplify teaching the Platz by first tiring your dog with several minutes of vigorous heeling. Don't exhaust the animal, but heel long enough and fast enough that the opportunity to lie down may look pretty good. Furthermore, if it's a warm, sunny day, heel in the sunshine and teach Platz in the shade. When pooch is tuckered out from the Fussing, demonstrate Platz three or four times in rapid succession. After the last presentation, permit him to remain grounded for a few minutes while you sit nearby, verbally marveling at his fine work.

"I Most Certainly Will Not!"

If that statement characterizes your dog's reaction to the idea of lying down on command or if he manifests the toaster syndrome (you take him down, he immediately pops up), apply the technique alluded to in chapter 5, "Training Guidelines," under the subsection "Same Chorus, Second Verse": Teach your pet that Platz directs, "Lie down *and* put your chin on your paws." The plan is to show more than is actually expected, causing the animal to focus any resistance on the command's secondary aspect rather than on its primary one. Later, settle for the act of lying down (i.e., don't worry whether he puts his head on his paws), which is what you were after in the first place.

To teach this procedure, first position the pinch collar as high on the neck as possible. This enables more pressure using less force. Next, get pooch on terra firma using whichever technique is easiest. Then, while grasping the leash right-handed close to the snap, put your left hand over the animal's withers (to prevent creeping), tell him, "No—I said, 'Platz!' " and tug the leash downward at a forward angle. At the same time, bring your left hand behind the recalcitrant's ears and push the head in the same forward-and-down direction. As he attempts to raise his head, which he will do, snap the lead down and forward while pushing on the back of his head/neck, accompanying this action with the same verbal censure. Stay with this method for several days. Pooch will likely continue to struggle over putting head on paws, but he'll be doing so from a horizontal position.

No, this is not how to teach the position were it the actual objective.

Too much compulsion exists to use it as a form of trick teaching. In that instance, a trainer would likely not be dealing with a resistant animal and certainly not until the dog had mastered Platz. Then one would proceed by using a separate command, placing a tiny food bit between the front paws, and reinforcement would entail minimal pressure.

Attitude Heightener

The foregoing subsection addresses canines that resist the Platz exercise out of pure stubbornness. Other dogs manifest an aversion to lying down not so much with an air of "No, I won't do that" as "I'd really rather not do that." It's as though the work seems demeaning, and while the command is obeyed, compliance is accompanied with an "Aw, shucks" attitude.

Raising a canine's opinion of the exercise is simple. Once the dog is responsive to the Platz command—that is, after he's past any physical rebellion and is going to ground reliably—direct, "Platz." As soon as he complies, praise, "Good Platz," a single time and casually drop a food bit in front of his nose. Present the treat in a very low key manner. The message is not one of a kickback but more that you discovered a snack in your pocket and wanted to share it. Should pooch ignore the gift, let it pass. Should he gobble it up, walk him a few steps and repeat the procedure. After a few days, begin to toss the food every other Platz. Later still, begin to present the treat randomly so that your pet is unable to predict when it might occur. Do *not* put the tidbit on the ground before the dog lies down—that could teach sniffing or crawling after lying down. Tossing it to him after he Downs teaches him to look up at you after Platzing.

"What If He . . . ?"

Once on the ground, a dog may attempt to roll onto his side or back submissively. Should yours do this, command "Platz," and as he reaches earth, commence to massage his back. Most dogs enjoy such petting, and it can't be done, of course, if the animal rolls over. This deflective technique often speaks to a sensitive canine far more productively than would sheer force.*

*I said earlier not to pet a dog's back, as doing so could cause him to rise. We're speaking here about submissiveness, however, and back rubbing seldom causes such a dog to get up.

If a dog rolls on his back when commanded to lie down, my practice is to accept the posturing for now.

"No Platz?" Through this technique even large animals can be quickly taken to ground.

Another deflective method is merely heeling your pet from the Down position very quickly, sometimes commanding "Fuss," just after commanding "Platz," and briefly praising "Good Platz—Fuss!" He'll soon see that you don't intend to wait for him to roll back over and hop up. Thus, he learns that it's to his advantage to Platz in a straight, on-paws posture.

The other option is to ignore the behavior for now. Don't insist that pooch hit the ground in a perfectly straight manner. If he flops over, be thankful he's not resisting you tooth and nail. The dog that effects such a posture is usually exhibiting submission to your dominance, which would be foolish to reject. He'll likely mature out of the tendency faster than it could be trained out. For now don't be concerned with precision. All we're after for the time being is that the dog makes no attempt to rise or otherwise challenge you. Should he try to get up either by sitting or standing, that constitutes a broken Stay and the animal must be summarily taken back down.

Uncommon Leash Usages

Two leash techniques exist for keeping a dog grounded. The first is to slip a portion of the lead under a front foot once pooch is in the Platz position. Should he attempt to rise, his action exerts corrective downward pressure via the pinned leash.

The second procedure is restricted to touch-sensitive dogs. Rather than inserting the lead under a foot (a touch-sensitive animal would pull the foot away), lay a coil or two of the leash across the front legs or across the back after he Platzes. This simple device can teach maintaining the Down position.

Platz Correction

Once you're convinced that pooch understands the new command, return the leash to your right hand. Should the animal refuse to Platz, correct by stepping onto the lead's slack with your left foot. Angle the force somewhat to the right rather than straight down so as not to risk spraining a leg. If you sense that the action may cause the dog to go for your leg or foot, use the right foot, although this is somewhat awkward to do. It's a bit safer, however, since your stationary left leg partially blocks your right from the animal's view and a dog that snaps in response to pressure usually does so toward movement.

How hard you step on the leash depends entirely on how tough a dog you're working. For some a toe tap does the job. Others may necessitate force sufficient to dig a crater, in a manner of speaking. As with any other first-time correction, if you're unsure how much force to apply, better to initially undercorrect than frighten through excessive pressure. Experiment on the side of caution, remembering that your next correction can always be tougher. Keep in mind that corrections are applicable only after it's clear that the dog understands the command.

An Effect of New Learning

There's an interesting phenomenon you might watch for. As new lessons are learned, any lingering resistance toward earlier teaching lessens. I've known a few dogs that, at this point, still harbored some defiance toward Automatic Sit. Once the Platz was introduced, however, the reluctance to automatically sit vanished. Why? Because pooch's attention was then occupied with the new work. If your pet still has misgivings about the Auto-Sit and teaching Platz doesn't have the side effect of decreasing reluctance to Automatic Sit at Heel, likely the Platz is being introduced too soon.

THE INTEGRATION PHASE

Initiate this stage after Platz has been learned. As you previously worked on Platz and heeling independent of one another, now begin to practice the exercises together. Accomplish this simply by commanding your pet to hit the ground seconds after an Automatic Sit during heeling. Referring to this particular instance, however, it's still unwise to direct Platz after every Automatic Sit. As mentioned earlier, pooch could infer that Auto-Sit is being replaced with Auto-Platz.

Hereafter, once your pal masters any new assignment, integrate it with others he already knows. Until the dog indeed comprehends any new lesson, however, continue to practice new work separate from already internalized lessons.

THE STAYS

This week's objective for the Sit-Stay and the Down-Stay is fifteen feet for two minutes. Practice both within an enclosed area to lessen the possibility of flight, thereby building the correct habit. To maintain control, either acquire a longer lead or attach a line to the six-foot leash. When using a thin line with a large or powerful dog, wear gloves to protect against friction burns.

To Lessen Anxiety

As Stay distance increases, some dogs display uneasiness born of insecurity. A long-range goal of any obedience program should be to heighten confidence. Ergo, don't travel beyond that point where pooch becomes nervous until he's at ease in the relative isolation.

Transferred Security

Canines left on a Stay often exhibit more confidence when in one body position than when in another. If your dog seems more at ease with a Sit-Stay than a Down-Stay, for example, initially lengthen durations and distances when the animal is in the preferred position. Add increases in time and distance later to the Stay position with which he's less comfortable.

"The Last Thing I Told You Was 'Stay!' "

Occasionally return to your dog, perhaps pet him, then leave again without further command. Since you've given no order to the contrary, pooch should maintain the Stay. Correct him if he breaks. When leaving the second time, however, don't do so in "heelinglike" manner, fraught with purpose. A forceful departure could cause confusion-based movement, in which case correction would be inappropriate—one doesn't pressure a confused dog. The intent is neither to deceive nor trick the animal nor to visually entice movement. The purpose is to demonstrate that your act of returning or coming nearby doesn't cancel the Stay.

I'm Often Asked . . .

"How do you deal with a dog that lies down during a Sit-Stay?"

Leash-lift him back up, accompanying the correction with a spoken "No—Stay!"

"How about the dog that lies down but hops into the sitting position as I move to correct him?"

If I take one step toward a dog to correct him, I'm going to do

Practicing a Resistance Stay. Notice that the lead is not pulled extremely tight and that verbal praise is occurring.

so regardless of what he does next (unless the animal is acting out of nervousness, fright or confusion). Otherwise, the dog is running the situation.*

Resistance Stays

Periodically attach your lead to both collar rings, having first pointed the prongs outward by turning the collar over. Command "Stay," and after stepping away a couple of paces, apply *mild*, momentary pulling pressure. Do *not* yank or tug the lead. Praise your companion as he endeavors to hold his ground. Correct gently should he move. A soft No—Stay will usually stop a canine that attempts to move in response to such pressure. He likely did so out of uncertainty rather than disobedience.

The technique is referred to as a Resistance Stay. Its rationale is to further define the meaning of Stay by causing the animal to have to work at doing it; by drawing attention to the job of maintaining position.

This method can be employed regardless of collar preference. When using a choke, attach the leash either to both rings or to only the dead ring and proceed as described above.

Competition Stays

If you plan to show in competition, you must return after any Stay from which you don't summon the animal by walking counterclockwise around him, halting in the Heel position.

The first time you effect this course of travel, pooch may break in response to the nearby, enticing leg movement. A dog might even decide you're trying to attract him. He could realize that by merely turning as you pass, he'd be in the Heel position.

The return routine is taught by practicing it while the dog is in a Sit-Stay and by initially walking *clockwise* around him. A dog is far less likely to abandon the Stay in response to this type of circling because it's not reminiscent of heeling, as is a counterclockwise course. Once he's accustomed to your walking clockwise around him, reverse the direction of travel.

*I recall watching a person whose dog was holding a Sit-Stay. After a short time, pooch started to lie down. The trainer advanced a step or two, the dog hopped up, so the trainer stepped back. A few seconds later, the dog started down again. The trainer moved toward the animal, which again popped up, and the trainer again retreated. It was an amusing minuet, one the tune-calling canine was enjoying immensely.

DISTRACTIONS

Function

As a dog begins to display understanding and proficiency, gradually add distractions to the training periods. The purpose is to create realistic situations that may lead pooch to stray from obedience. Continued responsiveness to commands should be acknowledged with sincere, if not effusive, praise. Loss of focus should be met with immediate correction.

Rationale

"Why tempt my pet to disobey?" That's a reasonable question from a novice's perspective (and it implies a seldom-acknowledged trap—which I'll tell you about momentarily—that experienced trainers sometimes overlook). The answer is that if contrived distractions can induce a dog to break, so can real ones. If your pet might stray from command in response to environmental influences, simulate such circumstances in controlled settings so you can communicate that he's to ignore such enticements and respond only to commands, specifically yours.

The trap alluded to is this: Trainers sometimes focus on contrived diversions to such a degree that they suggest the animals should imitate them. For instance, a handler tosses an object onto the ground while pooch is holding a Stay. Then, instead of ignoring the article, the person looks from dog to object several times. A canine could conclude that he's expected to take some action toward the article. Of course, if he does, the trainer corrects for the broken Stay, even though the dog's error resulted from faulty communication. In the foregoing example, the trainer would be wiser (and more forthright) to casually flip the object to one side and ignore it. The purpose of distraction work is to tell a dog he should respond to the trainer's commands, not to the environment's beckoning voices. It's not to say, "Figure out the situation as best you can, with no help from me." So teach by example. If another animal passes the training area, ignore it. If you divert attention to the interloper, your dog may justifiably imitate you. The question then would be, Which of you should be corrected?

Concept

The underlying idea is to turn up your radio, so to speak, louder than the environmental one broadcasting to pooch. Overcome distractional pressure by supplanting it with *attraction* from you. No, don't try to overpower with the decibel level of your voice or untoward force. Apply firm, steady and unyielding pressure to bring attention back to you. Simply standing between the dog and the distraction can block environmentally generated stress and communicate your goal. Pooch learns that during work he needn't be concerned with nearby happenings. Moreover, he learns over time that you won't place him in a situation that can hurt or threaten him. Long-term, this heightens trust in you.

Get Real

While visiting other instructor's training classes, I've seen "distraction work" conducted by aiming a radio-controlled toy car at dogs holding Stays. Any animal that moved was severely taken to task. Do such a thing with my dog and you'll lose a toy car, justifiably. If he doesn't take the thing out, I will.

A similar ploy I've witnessed is forcibly dropping a large metal garbage can very near a dog holding a Stay. Common sense causes pooch to move, and the "trainer" reinforces the animal's fear by applying a correction.

Unless real-world needs require that a dog maintain a Stay in the face of threatening mechanical objects or while the garbage is being picked up, stay with reasonable distractions. Remember who is at leash's end.

Reflection

Once he passed by a dog as it was being beaten, and pitying it, spoke as follows: "Stop and beat it not; for the soul is that of a friend."

Xenophone, of Diogenes

10

Third Week

HEEL ON LEASH AND AUTOMATIC SIT

Four simple yet effective techniques for improving heeling relate to starts, turns and pace changes.

The Turn Away

No law requires taking your first heeling step toward the direction you and pooch happen to be facing. Thus, as you command "Fuss," take your first step backward and to the right. This causes you to start walking in the direction nearly opposite the one you were facing. Since your left leg momentarily blocks the dog's path, he has to work at hurrying around it. Praise "Good Fuss," as he struggles to assume and maintain the Heel position.

Multiple About-Turns

An equally instructive variant is to perform double and triple about-turns in place. That is, as you make an about-turn, immediately do another, and another, without any forward steps between each. This technique heightens concentration on you by reminding pooch that your route can't be predicted and that his best interests are served by maintaining focus on you.

Zigzag Heeling

The third technique is to effect alternating right and left turns every third or fourth step, causing you to walk in a zigzag pattern. The dog that stays with you through these moves is excelling at very difficult work.

Uses of Speed Changes

Sporadic pace changes—in conjunction with turns or with straight-line heeling—are very effective in capturing and maintaining attention. I'm not referring to competition-style pace changes, whereby one walks normally for ten steps (for example), then runs for ten, normal for another ten, slow for ten and so forth. That's a heeling pattern, as opposed to irregular, instructive speed changes.

An example of *challenge-heeling* pace changes is several steps at normal speed, then an abrupt change to six steps at a slow rate, followed by fifteen at a fast pace (with a right turn after the first five steps), to ten normal steps, to three at slow, to stop. Of course, one needn't count steps or try to duplicate this arbitrary sequence. My intent is to illustrate the idea of making heeling sufficiently difficult to cause pooch to have to work at it.

Related is the notion of initiating steps at other than your usual pace. Begin at a run or at a slow pace. To do so is natural. Situations can cause you to go from stationary to a running or slow pace without beginning at normal walking speed. Acquaint your dog with this fact now, before a real event occurs.

Praise

When using any of these forms of *challenge heeling*, praise with utmost sincerity as your pet stays with you. He's having to work harder than you might suspect, and his efforts should be acknowledged. Practice of this nature increases heeling proficiency, but of equal importance, it strengthens the working bond.

THE PLATZ REVISITED

Sniff Ye Not!

Some canines are prone to sniff the area about them when in the Platz position. It's a natural, exploratory reaction. However, it can also be a method by which an independent animal tunes out the handler: "I'll lie down, but only because I want to sniff the area, not because you told me to." Regardless of motivation, though, the activity can lead to creeping. I once watched a Doberman creep at full sniff all the way across the ring at an obedience trial to the handler during the Down-Stays.

To correct the behavior, first command, "Platz." As pooch hits the ground and begins to sniff, flick your leash sideways and tell him, "No!— Platz!" In other words, an element of Platz is "No Sniffing!" Should the mild tug cause the animal to rise, block him with your hand across or just behind the withers.

THE STAYS

Lengthen the Stays to twenty-five feet for three minutes. Due to the increased time, reduce the number per session from four to two.

At some point while increasing distance, drop your long lead rather than deal with its cumbersome length. Flip the leash toward your direction of departure rather than merely discarding it in a heap near the dog. Should he make a run for it, sufficient slack is nearby to impede flight.

Dealing with the Potential Runner

If you sense that your dog may take off once you've dropped the lead, it's better to deal with the problem now than later. Retain your hold of the looped end when releasing the surplus, but unbeknownst to the animal. This ploy can often cause a calculating canine to conclude that the leash has been abandoned entirely; that he's free to depart for other activities.

Should the animal run, don't say anything, not one word. You've already said, "Stay." Should he choose to ignore the command, you needn't further warn about consequences. Merely brace yourself and allow the laws of physics to prevail. After he hits the end of the lead, bring pooch back to where you'd left him, apply a forceful Sit or Platz correction (depending on which posture you'd commanded) and depart again, affecting a somewhat bored, shaking-of-the-head, disgusted air, one that says you've seen it all before (even if you haven't).

Should you be working with a behemoth that you feel could yank you out of your sneakers, modify the procedure by correcting the dog after he takes one step. Tug the lead at a right angle to the direction of his intended path. Accompany the correction with a memorable diatribe, one that commences with "No!"

HAND SIGNAL—STAY

Begin to occasionally use the Stay hand signal in place of the spoken command. Then your pet can be commanded to Stay via the verbal command, the hand signal or both. Practice all three variations.

Hand-Signal Teaching Method

The hand signal for Stay is taught in much the same manner as the verbal command. Signal Stay by placing your right palm in front of the dog's eyes and step away briefly a few paces. It's initially helpful to continue holding your palm toward pooch for the entire time you're away.

Pooch probably won't break from position, even when first given this form of command. You've been teaching the signal for over two weeks by linking it with the spoken Stay. This is just the first time you didn't verbalize Stay.

Hand-Signal Maxims

When working with hand signals, it's consistent to maintain silence during subsequent praise or correction. To switch repeatedly from voice to signal to voice can confuse.

Once it's apparent your pet grasps the idea, it's a major error to withhold giving the sign until he happens to look your way. If you, as trainer, are about to give a signal but just then your dog looks away, don't wait until he (eventually) looks back before giving the command. Give it as you'd intended, correcting pooch forthwith should he move as or after you leave. The trainer decides when a command is to be given, not the dog.

Practice by giving the Stay signal and leaving normally. Should your pal attempt to depart also, correct for the broken Stay and immediately exit again. If the dog seems confused, clarify by signaling again as you leave the second time.

Purposes

The ideas are threefold: first, to teach the Stay hand-signal command; second, to show that the concept of hand signals unaccompanied by verbal commands exists; third, to reinforce that pooch must maintain focus on you when working.

First Signal?

A point I could have mentioned earlier may have more meaning now. This isn't the first signal you've taught. Granted, it's the initial hand signal, but introduction to signal work began when you taught Automatic Sit during on-leash heeling. Pooch learned to take your cessation of motion to be a signal to Sit.

OVER JUMP AT HEEL

Purposes

Three motivations underlie adding this activity: first, to acquaint your pet with the jump command Hup; second, laying the foundation for competition work (such as retrieving over a high jump), should such be your goal, and third, extending that training into practical activities, such as jumping into and from a vehicle, over an obstacle during field work and so forth; last, to bring some fun into heeling, which by now can be something of a semiboring function for both of you. Dogs generally love to jump, especially if the trainer demonstrably shares the enjoyment. Adding jumping to heeling work tells pooch that it can also be heeling fun. Not heeling play, mind you—heeling fun.

Initial Jump Height

Acquire a board three feet long by four to twelve inches wide. The width is dependent on pooch's height and physical condition. Though negotiating great heights isn't the aim, if you're working a large animal that you feel might not even notice a board in this size range, use a wider one, provided you *both* can jump over it without undue effort or risk.

Over Jump at Heel, with the accent on enjoyment.

Place the object lengthwise on the ground, propping it against some object (such as a construction block) so that the board rests on edge.

Over Jump at Heel—Teaching

Command, "Fuss," heel toward the board and command, "Hup," *as* (not before) your pet leaps over it. If possible, jump over the plank with *both* feet simultaneously instead of leaving the ground with one foot at a time or by merely stepping over the obstacle. This is admittedly a small element of technique, but your pet will respond with heightened enthusiasm if you propel yourself over the hurdle in this manner. If you want to know why, observe his style of jumping. When confronted by an object in his path, a dog goes around the obstacle or steps over it if he's able. He does so to be efficient. He leaps over the same obstacle from a sense of enjoyment. It's your job to instill this sense of delight, and the attitude can best be communicated by example.

Jumping Problems

Should pooch balk at the jump, encourage him over it but not through compulsion. An anxious canine tends to maintain his hold on terra firma, thereby feeling more secure. The primary purpose of this exercise is canine entertainment, and you'd have to talk for a long time to convince me that leash-dragging a dog into a situation he distrusts will heighten his animation or pleasure. Should your pet appear to want to try the jump but holds back anxiously, gently lift him over it. Then turn and heel over the obstacle while encouraging him to come across.

Should pooch attempt to go around the jump's left end, deflect intent by positioning that end against a fence, a building or a similar structure. That's preferable to verbal or physical censure. It avoids a spirit-dampening confrontation that may not be necessary. A dog that tries an end-run maneuver is likely nervous or merely taking the line of least resistance. Compulsion at that point could trigger fear or confusion.

Don't Stifle Drive

It's unwise at this point to heel toward a hurdle your pet has previously jumped, only to turn away from it at the last second. He'd likely jump across the obstacle even though you had turned from it, which would cause an undeserved correction. Yes, taking the jump in that instance represents anticipation, but setting your companion up at this early stage would be self-defeating. Putting a damper on a drive exercise in this context simply isn't done.

It's equally unsound to heel toward a jump that pooch has been over, only to slam on the brakes a step short of the object. At this stage, most dogs will blow the Automatic Sit, leading to an unprofitable correction and a resultant loss of drive.

Later, after much learning has taken place, either of the two preceding moves are proper. During these initial periods, however, no good purpose is served by their use.

Correct Working Height of a Jump

Keep the obstacle's height low during the teaching phase. Raise it over a period of several weeks to your pet's proper working height using additional or wider boards that combine as part of a formal structure. For noncompetition purposes, a jump equal to the dog's wither (shoulder) height is adequate.

Jump height can be a problem in terms of the amount of force that can safely be absorbed during landings. Very young canines and obese animals have no business taking jumps higher than half their wither height. Dogs suffering from hip or elbow dysplasia, osteochondritis dissecans, panosteitis or similar conditions should not be jumped, period. Doing so can exacerbate any of those conditions.

THE RECALL

Structure

The Recall ("Come to me") is similar to heeling in that both allow a dog to be with the handler. It is dissimilar in that Fuss requires pooch to be at your left side, while Here, used as the command word, teaches him to sit in front of and facing you after coming to you.

Pretraining

It's shrewd to precede any Recall instruction with a few days of Over Jump at Heel. This is one of those situations where a quasi-soundalike command can have a positive effect. Since most canines enjoy jumping, they come to perk up after a few days of such training when hearing the "H" sound in "Hup." Transfer of this lively attitude to the Recall often

150

occurs when the dog hears the "H" in "Here." Such sequencing and other factors enable teaching the Recall largely through drive techniques rather than through compulsion, which has been the principal teaching basis so far. The drive approach has the advantage of teaching pooch to come to you displaying an attitude of hardly being able to wait to get there. Often dogs are taught the Recall either out of sequence or through harsh methods. They come when they're called, yes, but their attitude is one of drudgery: Sigh— "I guess I've got to." I prefer that my dog come as though his tail were on fire. The command is Here, but the attitudinal message is "Now!" in the sense of granted permission to one enthusiastically awaiting it.

It's a Location

An important yet often misunderstood concept is that both the Fuss and Here commands allude to positioning. Remember, Fuss directs maintaining a constant position relative to the handler. Likewise, Here doesn't merely order coming to you: It directs pooch to sit in front of and facing you. Whether he'll come should never be allowed to develop into a question. If you take it for granted that he'll come when called, so will your dog.

"But . . . ?"

A beginning trainer could justifiably ask why a dog that comes when called is required to sit (or assume any position) at all. "If he comes to me, isn't that good enough?" The answer has two parts.

First, you want pooch thinking about what he's going to do when he arrives, not *if* he's going to arrive. That way, whether he'll come never becomes a speculative issue for him. Secondly, it's one thing to teach a dog to come, but it's another matter to keep him there. Without the Sit requirement (or a similar one), the animal may come, but often only to circle the handler a time or two and depart again. If a dog has no reason to remain, usually he won't.

True, your focused attention on your pet would usually be sufficient attraction to cause him to remain with you. That's provided you're working on obedience at the time. It's equally valid that a situation that necessitates calling your dog may cause your attention to be elsewhere during or soon after his arrival. Again, it's more conducive to canine learning to teach pooch to do (Sit, in this case) than it is to teach him not to do (run off after arriving). This procedure establishes and maintains control from the moment of calling your friend.

Teaching the Recall. Note the animation with which the Rottweiler explodes from the Sit-Stay position.

Use the Dog's Drives

A minor yet worthwhile teaching element in Recall training is initially staging practice so that your pet is consistently called to the general direction of his sleep area, as opposed to being called away from it. As mentioned in chapter 4, "Instincts and Drives," dogs have a drive to return home. Use it.

Teaching Method

Teach the Recall only to a Stay-sure animal. Otherwise, you may have to correct for premature movement at a time when you're trying to induce controlled movement.

Begin by commanding Stay. Leave pooch in the sitting position for now, not the Platz. Since the Recall teaches a dog to come to the trainer and Sit, most canines have an easier time learning the format when directed from a Sit to a Sit.

Step to the end of the six-foot lead, holding it left-handed. Endeavor to establish eye contact, freeze your entire motion for a beat, command "Here," and commence running backward. As pooch nears, stop and command, "Sit." As he Sits, praise, "Good Here—Sit." Stroke under the chin, causing him to look up at you. To praise a small dog, kneel rather than bend, the idea being not to intimidate, as can occur when looming over a dog.

The leash should remain slack throughout the procedure. There's no need to drag your pet to you. Your sudden movement elicits the response through the dog's sense of play (and, to a degree, prey) drive.

Fade out the Sit command over a few days, as you did when teaching the Automatic Sit at Heel and the Stay cue with Platz. Most canines learn the Sit portion of the Recall quite readily. Many assume the posture when nearing the handler even before the command can be given. The procedure by which the commanded Sit was taught created in your pet's mind an attitude of sitting when finding himself in a front and facing position.

As your companion catches on to the Recall concept, lessen the running-backward movement until it's no longer needed.

Lest Ye Go Splat

When employing the running-backward technique, be mindful of one caution: Know what is behind you. That warning may seem superfluous, but realize how easy it is to overlook the obvious when attempting to synchronize several mechanical and conceptual processes. During my first few months of teaching public obedience classes, I once exhorted an assemblage thrice over to "Know what is behind you!" Then, as though to accent the point, I called the dog I was working and dashed backward into a momentarily forgotten fence I'd erected days before. While the incident afforded those present a good chuckle, it startled the daylights out of my pet, and it didn't do me a lot of good, either.

Common Sense

When pooch arrives, yes, command "Sit," but no, don't take his head off if he does so slowly or crookedly. One does not call a canine and "reward" with punishment upon arrival. That just isn't done. Following such blatant mishandling, a dog with any sense won't come a second time, certainly not with any air of enthusiasm. Clumsy your companion into the Sit if you must, but barring out-and-out resistance, don't correct him into position.

How Straight is Straight?

Two deflective techniques for producing straight front-and-facing sits are effective with environmentally sensitive animals. Keeping in mind that the dog that swings his butt to one side as he sits generally does so to the same side, do Recalls along and very near fences or similar structures to the side pooch errs toward to block such movement and build the proper habit. The second method pertains to the leash. When calling a dog, the lead often hangs slightly to one side of the neck instead of straight down. This results in crooked sits as the dog tries to avoid the lead's pressure. Draping the leash over the other side just before Staying the animal often produces a straight sit.

Not More than Six Feet

Don't call from a starting distance greater than six feet this first week. By employing the running-backward technique, the dog will cover more distance than six feet (as well as learn a quick start). Calling over longer distances prematurely by using a longer leash can teach the animal to weave and zigzag.

In the Beginning

For now, don't use the formal Here to call your dog when he's off leash. Were you to do so and were he not to respond correctly, the effect of your not being able to back up the command could suggest that he may disregard Here anytime it suits.

Reminder

As with all commands, the dog's name is not to be used with Here. During high-stress situations (such as obedience competition), the name can be an ace if it hasn't been overused during training. Since AKC rules allow name usage during competition (except during the Utility Dog hand-signal routine), should pooch look away just as you're about to summon him, you can recapture attention by using the name before commanding, "Here."*

Nuts and Bolts

There are four integral elements to the Recall. First, control is established with the Stay command. Second, this control, or contact, is extended over time and distance by virtue of your departure. Third, a sense of anticipatory excitement is created in the animal through eye contact and body language. That you aren't moving around (as you normally are during a Stay) but are stationary and facing your pet will probably capture attention by communicating a feeling of tension, in the sense that "something's different, something's coming." Last, this suppressed canine excitement is vented through his dynamic response to the Here release.

Not Yet

The Finish exercise, whereby a canine returns to the Heel position when commanded, shouldn't be included yet. After praising for the Recall, *you* should return to the Heel position rather than trying to reposition your pet. Not only would that be too much to teach during one period; the effect of teaching the Finish simultaneous with teaching the Recall could suggest that pooch should return to the Heel position automatically

*The rules concerning Schutzhund obedience, incidentally, forbid using the dog's name during competition.

after arriving. Remember, *Canis familiaris* is behaviorally patterned. For him to infer that he should automatically return to the Heel position could seem reasonable. It might represent just another automatic function, such as the Automatic Sit during Heeling, the Automatic Stay as an element of Platz and the Automatic Front-and-Facing Sit during a Recall.

Behaviors to Watch For

When first shown this exercise, a minority of canines can mistake their handler's animation as an engraved invitation for hilarity and high jinks. This is often displayed by the animal's attempt to run past the trainer, often to the person's right.

If your pet pulls this bit of tomfoolery, deflect by blocking his path and directing, "No!—I told you, 'Here!' " Should the dog later try the same maneuver, even though you've demonstrated the correct procedure, you're likely dealing with a form of disrespect that should be brought to a screeching halt forthwith. Permit the illusion that he'll be able to blow past you. As pooch nears, tug the lead in the direction he's going, continuing the move into a counterclockwise turning of the dog so that he settles sitting in front of you. (This motion will be clockwise should the animal try to pass on the left.) Follow with "I told you, 'Here!' " The technique requires timing more than strength; the idea isn't to overcome the dog's momentum but to redirect it.

A firmer correction is allowing your pet to zip past you, digging your heels in and bracing yourself. Let him hit leash's end with whatever degree of force his momentum generates. Then pull the animal to you, command "Sit," and verbalize, "*I* told you, 'Here.' " Sure, these are semitough corrections, but when a dog defies authority, better to be firm now than to have to really land on him later.

Confusion

A less troublesome canine tendency to be alert for is that when commanded to Sit, some dogs attempt to do so in the Heel position instead of in front of and facing the handler. Should this occur, don't reflexively assume your pal is being disobedient. It can be the sign of a pretty bright animal. Such a dog should not be sternly corrected for initiative. He should be guided to the proper location, clarifying what Here defines.

Another deflective approach is initially positioning yourself to the right of a solid structure when calling your dog. He'll be blocked from going to the Heel position and can learn the correct procedure through habit formation.

Reversed Heeling

The technique of Reversed Heeling can greatly aid in teaching pooch to sit close and straight in front. Command, "Stay" (with pooch in the Sit position) and place yourself in front of and facing the animal from only a few inches away. The result is to put him in the ideal front-and-facing position, where he should be after being called. Command, "Here," and take three or four quick steps backward. As you halt, command, "Sit." Praise, "Good Here—Sit," as he complies. Use only minimal leash pressure to maintain your pet's position relative to yours. The idea is to demonstrate that whether you call him across a great distance or from only inches away, pooch is to assume and maintain the Here location, just as he does the Heel position when commanded, "Fuss."

The Reversed Heeling technique also makes life easier by enabling reinforcement of the correct front position while in a controlled setting. Attempting to Sit a large, exuberant dog that is on a dead run without the use of force (and at the expense of a resultant loss of drive) can be quite a chore indeed.

No Bending Allowed

A common error in technique is bending forward when summoning a dog. Maintain your normal posture. If you feel compelled to alter your posture, bend slightly *backward*: This stance can encourage a dog to come. Bending forward often has the reverse effect—it tends to keep a dog back, or slow his approach, since the domineering position can suggest you're about to fall upon him. Objects above canine eye level usually inhibit.

Don't Do It

A competition technique uses a different Stay command when the handler intends to call his pet. Under such a system, a Stay command supposedly tells a dog that he won't be called, while a Wait cue (for instance) advises the animal that he'll be summoned. It's an unsound, unwarranted practice. It makes marginal sense in people terms, but Recalls apply to dogs, not humans.

At a recent AKC obedience trial, a handler was using the technique of two separate Stay commands. While facing her animal from across the ring, the judge directed, "Call your dog." Before the handler responded, the animal ran to her. What happened, of course, was that the Wait cue facilitated anticipation of the handler's next move, and pooch took the judge's cue as confirmation. The method foreshadows the next event. Because canines are behaviorally patterned, it's seldom a good idea to suggest what will occur next. Moreover, the dog who doesn't know what the next command will be tends to pay more attention so as not to miss anything. Besides, Stay means "remain motionless until commanded otherwise." That should say it all. To add a second command only risks confusion.

BE SURE YOU'VE TAUGHT A LESSON

If you'd enjoy an insight as to how a dog "thinks," do the following sequence once. Command, "Platz." Praise, "Good Platz." After your friend has been grounded a few seconds, command "Sit." Command "Sit," *only once*, without any accompanying body motion, and *don't* use the dog's name. Most importantly, do *not* (repeat: *not*) Sit-correct the animal should he fail to respond by hopping into position.

If pooch sits as commanded, praise "Good Sit." If he doesn't, move out with "Come on, pup" or the like and tell him how truly fine he is, taking his mind off the event.

Since your pet knows by now to Sit on command, to hold a Sit-Stay, to Sit automatically at Heel and to Sit automatically in front of and facing you after a Recall, isn't it reasonable to assume that he'd hop into the sitting position as commanded? It would be if you were you training an animal possessing human thought patterns, but that's a dog at leash's end, and dogs simply don't process information that way. Most canines don't generalize certain types of learned behaviors. That's why your pet likely didn't Sit in the foregoing example, unless he's one in about seventy-five that acted out of confusion or unless you moved, flicked your leash or used his name when commanding, "Sit." If you want your pet to Sit from the Platz position, you must teach the move. (Which, incidentally, is easily done by commanding Sit simultaneous with taking a very quick half-step forward. He'll raise into the Sit position in response to your sudden start-and-stop movement.)

The moral is, should pooch fail to respond to any training you might devise in the future, be absolutely certain you've shown him what he needs to know to do the work. When a teaching scheme goes awry, it's usually because a step linking part of the sequence with those preceding it has been passed over.

A PONDERANCE

A premise on corrections needs reiterating. Some self-anointed experts who are perhaps better wordsmiths than trainers take the view that all dogs must be corrected with equal severity. This only bespeaks the ignorance of those who should know better. I repeat a thesis stated earlier: Any correction should represent force that is one inch tougher than the dog, no more. The notion that every canine is a hardheaded, rebellious ne'er-do-well requiring constant, unrelenting and extreme pressure before he can join the legion of the truly trained comes right off the stable floor.

Force can accomplish much, and it's an integral part of dog training, but without applications of TLC, the job remains undone. Excessive force results in fear training, which is not only a moral crock; it doesn't work. The first time a dog thus conditioned is in a situation he fears more than he does the "trainer," the lessons go right out the window. The dog has learned—moreover, he's been taught—to avoid the greater fear.

Reflection

The more I see of men, the more I admire dogs.

Madame Roland

Teaching the Inside Finish.

An alternate manner of teaching the Inside Finish.

11

Fourth Week

THE RECALL

Distance

Gradually lengthen Recall distance to fifteen feet. To ensure control, use a longer leash or attach a line to the primary lead. Continue to call pooch only from Sit-Stays. Increased distance is sufficient change for now.

"Catch!"

A technique for increasing Recall fire is spitting a food bit to pooch after he sits in the Here position. Liver bits (used in conformation baiting) work well, as do hot-dog chunks. When adding this reinforcer to the repertoire, bear three thoughts in mind.

First, the procedure remains effective only so long as it's performed at irregular intervals. Don't use it every time you call your pet. Lacking the element of mystery—"Will there be a treat for me?"—a canine learns to take the practice for granted, and the technique can lose attraction. Second, introduce the idea only to a hungry animal, not to one that has recently eaten. Third, the dog must first be taught to catch expectorated food. Start by teaching pooch to catch tidbits tossed from your hand, not allowing him to pick up uncaught pieces. Next, flip the snack while holding it near your mouth. Then bring the food bit to your mouth, move your hands slightly away and spit the morsel to your friend. Last, take the tidbit in your mouth, put your hands at your sides and *whock-toohy* the treat in his direction.

While the idea of spitting treats at your dog may seem bizarre at first, consider how effective a conditioning device this will be for strong eye contact. After a while you can get used to anything, and to your dog, you are the fountain from which all blessings flow!

Not Yet

Two Recall applications that shouldn't be introduced to a competition animal until basic titles have been earned are calling him from a Stay held among other dogs or calling him from out of sight. The effects of such learning could spell disaster in a ring setting where neither event is required.

THE FINISH

Attributes

A dog Finishes by moving from the front-sit location to the Heel position; from the Here location to the Fuss position.

In competition, the Finish immediately follows the Recall. When teaching the exercise, however, whether your goal is to be in the ribbons or to have a well-mannered pet (or both), practice the two activities separately, lest the animal infer he should Finish automatically.

Most dogs learn the Finish either in a few minutes or about a week, the majority winding up in the former group. If your pet has learned Fuss is a location, not merely a cue to accompany you during a stroll, he'll emerge in the few-minute category.

Two Styles and a Variation

There are two basic Finish patterns. The Outside Finish (also known as the Go-Around, or Military Finish) has the animal circling past the handler's right side and behind him on the way to the Heel position. The Inside Finish has pooch moving to Heel by stepping forward and to his right, then turning 180 degrees counterclockwise to arrive at the handler's side. Some dogs make the move by pivoting on their front legs and swinging butt first into the Heel position. A third version, the Flip Finish, is an Inside variation: The dog jumps upward, spins 180 degrees while airborne and lands sitting at Heel.

Inside Advantages

The Inside Finish is easier to teach, and it's easier for most canines to learn. They perceive the goal more quickly, perhaps because the route from the front-and-facing location to the Heel position is more direct. Less travel is required.

Another built-in plus of the Inside Finish is that it facilitates—indeed, causes—pooch's eyes to remain on you during the maneuver. The Inside technique can also foster a quicker working attitude, as the move can be effected faster and dogs generally relish executing flashy movements.

Outside Disadvantages

The Outside Finish takes longer to perform, if for no other reason than more ground must be covered. It's somewhat harder to teach (especially for novice trainers) and often finds the dog sitting behind and perpendicular to the handler. Because the Outside Finish necessitates more movement, more can go wrong in its performance.

Also, the Outside Finish generates more chance for lost contact between handler and dog. I once observed an exhibitor at an obedience trial who, after commanding his charge to Finish, found himself bereft of dog. The animal had been schooled in the Go-Around maneuver, but this time he didn't fulfill the ''Around'' part: The dog merely went—past the owner's right side and out of the ring. Surely, this could occur during the Inside Finish, but since neither the dog nor the handler is ever out of the other's sight during its execution, it's far less likely.

But if it Works for You and Yours . . .

Though I lean toward the Inside Finish, I've encountered more than one dog that manifested an immediate and clear understanding of the exercise coupled with a tendency to perform it in Go-Around fashion. These dogs seemed drawn to the side opposite the one intended. If faced with this situation, don't fight success. Should pooch demonstrate a pro-

Teaching the Outside or Go-Around Finish.

clivity for executing an exercise in a style different from the one planned, don't dissuade him so long as the end result is acceptable.

Teaching Either Style

To teach either the Inside or the Outside Finish, begin with pooch sitting at Heel. Command "Stay," and step in front of and facing him from a few inches. The idea is to simulate the end of a Recall with your pet in the Recall-Sit location. Then follow the steps outlined below for the preferred Finish style.

Inside Finish—Teaching Methods

To teach the Inside Finish, control the leash left-handed. Make eye contact, command "Fuss," and quickly step backward and then forward with your *left* foot. The right foot should remain stationary. Leash-guide and body language pooch slightly past your left side, turning him toward the Heel position. Praise "Good Fuss," as he sits. Phase out leg movement as your pet catches on.

An alternate teaching method is following the Fuss command with a *mild* leftward bump from the inside of your right knee to the dog's left shoulder. The effect is to brush the animal sufficiently to the left that you can leash-guide him into the Heel position. The technique is applicable in the case of larger canines that seem resistant or confused by more conventional teaching means. Like before, as the dog sits at Heel, praise "Good Fuss."

Outside Finish—Teaching Method

To teach the Outside Finish, hold the leash right-handed. Make eye contact, command "Fuss," and quickly step backward and then forward with your *right* foot. The left foot shouldn't move. Use leash pressure and body language to guide the dog clockwise around yourself, passing the leash behind your back to your left hand. Praise "Good Fuss," as pooch sits in the Heel position. Fade out leg movement as your pal learns.

A Commonality

An aspect of technique for teaching either Finish style is stepping backward coincident with commanding, "Fuss." The idea is to cause pooch to move forward in response to leg movement; to attract him toward the Heel position without using force. Pulling the lead could have the effect of causing the dog to try to remain in place. As stated in chapter 8, "First Week," under "The Sit—Preferred Teaching Method," ". . . when one leash-pulls a dog in a given direction, the animal reacts by pulling in the opposite direction." While this canine tendency is to our advantage for teaching the Sit, employing the same approach—pulling the dog into position—for teaching the Finish would be to disavow the principle. Since your pet is accustomed by now to responding to Fuss with movement, especially when your leg moves as the command is given, capitalize on that learned response. Yes, you're stepping backward, but from the dog's perspective, the movement appears forward.

A Problem

While the foregoing leg-movement technique for teaching the Finish is effective as well as humane, sometimes its use leads to a difficulty: The dog doesn't move until the trainer's leg does. It's understandable from a canine view—the animal is waiting for the confirming "signal" to Finish. If you see this "Move your leg and I'll Finish" response in your dog, signifying willingness and a desire to do right, don't resort to harsh compulsion to overcome the problem. Communicate intent by turning your upper body in the direction you want pooch to go, along with *mild*, quick-tug-and-release, suggestive leash pops. Also, giving the command more than once—that is, talking to the dog—to aid understanding is more than permissible during this teaching stage. As he catches on and moves to the Heel position, praise your pal to reaffirm his decision.

Don't Misread Pride as Disobedience

Sometimes, when first arriving at the Heel position, a dog is so pleased with himself he forgets to sit. He may not even realize it's expected. As mentioned in chapter 10, "Third Week," under "Be Sure You've Taught a Lesson," most dogs don't generalize certain forms of behavior. If it's your pet I'm talking about, don't correct him for failure to read your mind. Show him the Finish and command, "Sit." He'll catch on soon enough without being knocked about.

Flip Finish—Overview

Unlike the traditional Finishes, not every dog can easily learn the Flip, nor is every trainer able to teach it. Moreover, I've met owners who felt that this style of Finish was unsuitable or impractical for their animals, usually owing to size, coordination, skeletal attributes or temperament.

Some people feel that the Flip is for smaller dogs, that it's inappropriate for the larger breeds. While I respect this opinion, I disagree with it. I've taught the Flip to several medium-sized to large canines, from English Springer Spaniels to Golden Retrievers to Doberman Pinschers to Great Pyrenees. Given the animal's obvious delight in executing the move, the term *inappropriate* seems irrelevant.

Sometimes referred to as the *Poodle Flip*, this style is as related to canine personality and temperament as to the level of intelligence and trainability (two traits that aren't always equally present in the same dog, incidentally). Mastery depends on the animal's natural tendencies and levels of self-esteem, trainer motivation and rapport. Unlike the conventional Finishes, mechanical techniques alone won't always produce the desired result or reliability. A dog uncomfortable with the move (or with any other) or with his situation will never perform it *reliably* unless discomfort is first eased.

Flip Finish—Teaching Methods

First teach the Inside Finish, the intent being for it to serve as a foundation for teaching the Flip. It's often easier to modify the Inside style once a dog has mastered it than to teach the Flip outright.

The exception to this approach occurs with the dog that not only grasps immediately the function and purpose of the Inside Finish but also seems naturally inclined to perform it in Flip fashion. With some dogs, the move appears to be natural. While that characterization may stretch the word's meaning, if you observe the tendency in your pet, go with it. Skip over the steps involved in teaching the Inside Finish. Otherwise, you risk not only boring the animal but loss of what you've already got. In such a fortunate situation, concentrate on accenting that which already exists.

Once your pal is versed in the Inside Finish, teaching the Flip can be accomplished using a board equal in width to one-half the animal's wither height. Set the board on edge and heel toward it, as though you were going to jump over it. As you near the obstacle, slow to a stalking pace and stop within a couple of inches of it. Command, "Stay" (sitting), and step over the board. Align yourself in front of and facing your companion but with the plank between you. Command, "Fuss." This method can easily develop the Flip Finish, as the dog must jump over the board to reach the Heel position.

An English Springer Spaniel named Jackie and a Golden Retriever named Sundance, each performing the Flip Finish. (*Note:* The photograph of the Golden Retriever is courtesy of Bill and Barb Ziegler.)

Another technique for suggesting and enhancing the Flip is simply commanding it from the Platz rather than from the Sit position. A fast worker will often come off the ground so quickly that his speed leads him to hop into the Heel position, a mannerism one can heighten through animated praise and gestures.

Before closing this section, know that compulsion-based methods for teaching the Flip exist. Representative of these are leash swinging and knee blasting a dog into the Heel position. I neither use nor recommend such amateurish treatment. While some characterize such methods as *proper instructive modes*, my choice of words is ego-sponsored abuse of a helpless animal. Your dog's friendship and trust are far more important than any performance enhancement, especially one so peripheral as the Flip Finish.

Fuss = Fuss

Some trainers use a Finish command other than the one used for heeling. If the approach works for you, fine. For the dog that has learned that Fuss is a precise position, however, a second command seems not only superfluous but risks muddying the waters. It can pointlessly complicate a simple process.

Why Bother?

Some owners question the need for any Finish. "He's only a house dog—why bother?" It's true: No screaming need exists for teaching a Finish to a noncompetition animal. Should one prefer to teach returning to heel as part of the Recall, that's his or her prerogative. However, there's no good reason *not* to teach the Finish to a "pet only" animal. The exercise has the side effect of reinforcing Fuss's true meaning (that it refers to a specific location) while stimulating canine gray matter. Even for a "mere house pet," Finish advantages outweigh the extra-time-and-effort disadvantages.

Besides, it's impressive. After pooch is skilled in performing the Finish around distractions, demonstrate the move for friends. Listen to the comments. "My Gawd! Did you see *that*?" Folks may even ask your help with their dogs.

OUT-OF-SIGHT STAYS

Now add the concept of leaving your companion's sight during Stays. As was the goal for first-week Stays, don't be gone more than a minute and build to that time gradually.

Technique

Out-of-Sights are easier taught by disappearing immediately, as opposed to walking a long distance before vanishing. The dog whose handler disappears quickly feels more secure than if the person fades at a long distance. Select a hiding place where you won't throw shadows and where wind direction won't carry your scent to pooch. Lessen confusion potential by using both voice and signal for Stay.

Insecurity Is Not Disobedience

Be cognizant that with a dog that has been Stay steady but breaks during Out-of-Sights, insecurity is more likely the cause than disobedience. If your pet seems anxious about this modified Stay, skip it for now and reintroduce it later when he's more secure.

Some Call Them Snitches

Teaching Out-of-Sights is easier with the assistance of a "fink" whose job is covertly cueing you should pooch transgress. Communication must be subtle: a cough, dropping a hat, etc.

Vary said fink and cue at least daily, lest the dog see and hear too much. More than once I've seen a dog holding a Sit-Stay lie down after the trainer disappeared; pooch heard the helper's hiccup (or whatever) and hopped back into the Sit before the handler could return. Obviously, a canine can learn that a helper's sound or gesture means the trainer is returning. Dogs are accurately defined as dumb animals because they lack speech abilities, but don't infer that they're stupid. They aren't.*

---

*Laurens Van Der Post penned as moving a statement as I've read about "dumb" animals in The *Night of the New Moon*, (New York: Fawcett, 1981):

> I had so often in the past seen dumb domesticated animals in Africa, so aware of the secret intent of people who had bred and reared them, and earned their trust, that they could hardly walk, knowing they were being led to a distant place of slaughter.

Teaching Out-of-sight Stays.

BACKSLIDING

In a phrase, this phenomenon is canine temporary amnesia. It occurs when a dog has been doing well, and then, out of the blue—often between the third and fourth training weeks—he seems to have forgotten everything, perhaps including his name.

As it occurs about one time in four, the odds are you won't have to contend with the problem. However, if one fine day you take pooch out and he lies down in response to Sit and stays when commanded, "Fuss," and so forth, put the leash away for three to five days. By then the difficulty will have passed on its own. In the interim, play with your friend daily but avoid command work. Don't resort to corrections—they only frighten during this time. They don't speed the process.

Reflection

I am secretly afraid of animals—of all animals except dogs, and even some dogs. I think it is because of the us-ness in their eyes, with the underlying not-us-ness which belies it, and is so tragic a reminder of the lost age when we human beings branched off and left them: Left them to eternal inarticulateness and slavery. "Why?" their eyes seem to ask us.

Edith Wharton

12

Fifth Week

THE RECALL

Speed

Sometimes as distance increases, speed decreases. If you're seeing signs of this, raise the velocity before lengthening distance farther.

One way to speed Recalls is to call the dog over long distances and walk slowly toward him while clapping your hands. A second helpful technique is just the reverse: Call pooch over a great distance and—as he starts to come to you—run away. Which method will work best with your pet is something only you can decide through experimentation with both.

Another technique for speeding Recalls requires the help of four or more people. Position them in a corridor setting: two groups located ten feet from the line along which you'll call your dog. Instruct that the instant he begins to come out of the Stay in response to Here, they're to react with applause and cheering, "Good Here!" Be aware that such commotion inhibits some animals at first. If you see the effect occurring in your pet, quell the mob a bit.

In most cases, group approval brings out the ham in a dog. This can happen to the extent that the Sit is less than perfect. Should that occur, don't trouble yourself about it for now—work on straightening out such minor concerns once the animal is accustomed to the noisy encouragement. Remember, we're working on Recall speed, not the Sit. When working on a problem, concentrate on one aspect at a time.

Attitude

Several ways exist for instilling and maintaining a positive canine outlook toward the Recall. Most have to do with the expectation the trainer radiates when calling the dog and the manner of praise once the animal arrives. If one merely goes through the motions, so will pooch. If you truly have feelings for your pal and can effectively communicate pleasure in having him join you, he'll run to you quickly and directly. Given proper bonding, a good dog can know no other way.

THE FINISH

Combine the Finish with the Recall if pooch has mastered both exercises. Should your companion be having problems with either, delay integration until he's proficient.

Anticipation

Once shown that the Finish follows the Recall, some dogs anticipate the Fuss command. Often such behavior is indicative of intelligence and initiative—it's seldom born of disobedience. Nonetheless, pooch cannot be allowed to act upon his estimation of the next command. That can be as detrimental as not responding to the command at all. In either situation the animal is calling the plays, and that's simply not obedience.

Should a dog repeatedly anticipate the Finish, deflect by temporarily dropping the exercise. Concentrate on reinforcing Here's meaning. When next combining the routines, if the animal still Finishes without command, block him and command, "No—Here!" Then reinforce further with Reversed Heeling (see chapter 10, "Third Week"). Another tack is to command, "Platz," a few seconds after the dog arrives and sits. (But don't command, "Platz," the instant pooch appears—he could infer that he's now supposed to always hit the ground upon arrival.) If he knows to Sit from the Down position, next command, "Sit," and then to Finish, or command the Finish from the Down position. The purpose is to vary the pattern so he's unable to predict the next command.

Should the animal radiate stubbornness—"I'll return to the Heel

Notice the flank is merely touched, not grasped.

position when *I* want!''—correct him back to the Here location by stepping backward (to clear an area for him) simultaneous with yanking the lead to your right and then toward yourself. The idea is to turn the animal in a semicircle from your left side to a point in front of yourself. As with all such corrections, accompany the move with ''No,'' adding the admonition ''I told you, 'Here!' ''

STAND-STAY

Stays, especially prolonged ones, are best applied to the Sit or Down position because they're more comfortable. It's wise to teach the Stand, however, simply for mental discipline. It's also handy for grooming.

Teaching Method—Small Dogs

With the smaller dog, the Stand is easiest taught by first commanding, ''Sit,'' then applying a light, left-handed tap under the midsection as you command, ''Wait.'' Once standing, stroke the front and center of the back in a firm, petting motion. The dog will push against the enjoyable pressure, thereby keeping himself in the Stand posture. Hand signal Stay—don't command the *S*tay verbally if you don't have to (the ''S'' sound could cause pooch to Sit)—and once he seems secure in the new position, move away a step or two for a few seconds.

Teaching Method—Medium to Large Dogs

The larger dog generally learns the Stand more easily while moving at heel. A finger tap to the left flank when commanding ''Wait'' often freezes a canine in his tracks. He might momentarily glance leftward to see what touched him, but attention can easily be regained by petting the head's right side. Don't exert leash pressure—that would cause him to Sit.

A Caution

Be sure to work with the outside flank, not the inside one. That is, with pooch in the Heel position, target the left flank, the one away from you. Touching the inside flank can cause a dog to spin away. This reaction isn't possible when the animal is touched on the outside flank as your leg blocks him. Also, with some canines, touching a flank can incite aggres-

Two methods to facilitate teaching the Stand.

177

sion. Tapping the outside flank is safer—by the time the dog turns toward the pressure, your hand should have moved away. Don't ever grasp a flank to teach the Stand. That can cause pain—the flank is highly sensitive—and can result in being bitten.

Reinforcements

As soon as pooch stands, praise "Good Wait." A gentle toe touch under the midsection can help maintain the Stand. A second leash looped under the stomach area can also be useful, as can hand pressure on the front of a stifle (upper rear leg).

Perspective

The Stand's objective isn't endurance. The Sit- and the Down-Stays are practiced in minutes; the Stand in seconds. One shouldn't use this (or any) Stay at the vet's office if the visit might be painful or unsettling. Such is not obedience's purpose.

INFORMAL COMMANDS

These are casual cues that require varying degrees of immediate compliance, owing to their nature. One is "Come with me" or "Come on," which communicates the notion of the two of you taking a relaxing constitutional. Without such a command you have nothing but strict heeling for getting around, which isn't always desirable. Your dog doesn't have to maintain the Heel position or Sit when you halt (though he may if he wishes), and he may walk on either side or even slightly ahead of or behind you. He's not to drag you along, however, nor may he leave your general area.

Another informal cue is "Go lie down," which means just that. The animal needn't immediately smack the ground and rivet constant attention on you, but neither is he permitted to wander about the house or yard for a half an hour before complying.

Some other informal commands and their translations:

"Give it" (Give me the article you have in your mouth.)
"C'mere" (Come here, but not in formal Recall context.)
"Move" (Remove yourself from my path.)

WEEKS 6, 7, 8, 9, 10, AND SO ON . . .

For many the material covered in the preceding lessons will prove adequate. For others it will serve as an appetite whetter and a springboard toward more advanced work. My hope is that in either case, you and your dog will continue to learn about one another and to grow.

Reflection

If you pick up a starving dog and make him prosperous, he will not bite you. That is the principal difference between a dog and a man.

Mark Twain

13

Dog Tricks

THIS CHAPTER is in the Companion Obedience section because tricks are as relevant to companionship as formal lessons. Trick training can raise communicative ability because force isn't an available teaching element. It necessitates rapport at a level beyond strict obedience. "Tricks can be a useful and entertaining addition to your dog's education. . . . Do you think tricks are just silly and useless? Read on and surprise yourself."*

Books have been written about trick training. While this chapter doesn't intend to rival them or present complex routines, it offers enough material to provide more than just heeling, sits and stays, so to speak, to share in and enjoy.

General Notes

Here are six guidelines about trick training.

Like formal obedience, praise is essential. It's what pooch is working for. The more sincerely one can communicate approval and delight, the quicker the dog will catch on and the more thoroughly you'll both appreciate and take pride in his efforts.

*Dog Tricks—Teaching Your Dog to be Useful, Fun, and Entertaining, by Captain Arthur J. Haggerty and Carol Lea Benjamin, from the Introduction (New York: Howell Book House, 1978).

Unlike formal obedience, cueing (commanding) more than once is permissible, especially during the initial instructive stages. Trick work's objective is fun, not rigid precision.

As with any form of training, teach only one new trick at a time. Showing a dog too many things during a single session risks confusion.

Don't labor over any lesson. To go on and on during a session can bore and frustrate. While twenty to thirty minutes of obedience is proper for an experienced dog, more than seven or eight minutes of trick teaching is too much.

Teaching is easier with an obedience-trained canine. Not only is pooch under control; he'll sooner perceive that you're trying to say something. He's learned you have things to communicate.

Tricks are presented here in a definite teaching sequence. Each new lesson builds to some degree on ones before it. This isn't to say you must teach each and every trick presented but that if you're interested in items two, five and seven, for instance, teach them in that order.

Shake Hands (Paws)

This is the old standby. Shake cues a dog to raise a front paw, presenting it to the person with whom he is to shake. Canines enjoy the activity because it affords physical contact with their family. Dogs like to touch, and this trick provides an outlet for that need. Moreover, once pooch has mastered the gesture, don't be surprised should he initiate it from time to time by approaching you, sitting and offering a paw. Should he do so, gently accept the foot and praise "Good Shake."

To teach this trick, command, "Sit-Stay," and kneel in front of your companion. Command "Shake" while lightly finger tapping the back of a front leg. This is best accomplished by accenting the leg opposite your hand—if you use your right hand, target the left leg. In any case, concentrate on one leg to the exclusion of the other. Don't grasp the paw tightly—hold it gently. If your pet seems uncertain of what is expected, gently lift the foot while praising, "Good Shake." Then release the paw and repeat the process. He'll catch on in time. Repetition plays a significant role in trick teaching.

Use Shake not just because of the shaking-hands connotation but because it sounds like Stay, which is what a dog must do to perform the trick. This is an instance in which a soundalike is helpful.

The basis for kneeling in front of pooch is twofold. First, the position is more initimate and less inhibiting than standing and bending at the waist. Second, points would be deducted were your competition dog to end a Recall pawing at your leg. If not taught to shake when you're standing, there's less chance he'll do so when you aren't kneeling or seated.

Don't be surprised if your pet seems reticent to shake with strangers. Some animals show understandable disinterest in contact with other than pack members (family). I've known dogs that resented such intrusion to the extent that when a stranger attempted to grab a paw in a friendly manner, the person was nearly bitten. While one could argue that the dog's temperament is suspect, it's doubtful that such theoretical discussions would be of interest to a bite victim. Should your pet seem disinclined to contact someone he doesn't feel close to, don't force the issue. Stress has no place in tricks; it defeats the original purposes of intimacy, contact and fun.

The Kiss

This is perhaps the easiest taught trick. Pooch learns to respond to "Kiss" with a slurp to your cheek. It's assumed that yours is a friendly, outgoing dog—one with questionable temperament might snap—and that you aren't averse to canine licking.

In many cases, to teach this stunt, one merely needs to place his or her cheek near the animal's muzzle and say, "Kiss." To enhance the response or teach it to a hesitant animal, spot a light coating of butter on your cheek and draw pooch's attention by putting your face near enough for him to smell. Curiosity and your pet's olfactory organ will take care of the rest. Your response of "Good Kiss, Good Kiss" cements the learning.

"Do You Love Me?"

An extension of "The Kiss," this trick is among my dog's favorites. My protection-trained Doberman jumps upward toward me and bestows a quick slurp on my cheek. My smaller pet, a seven-pound, fuzzy crossbreed of indeterminate origin, responds by jumping as high as he's able, to be caught and cuddled. Both feel this trick is one of life's more pleasurable activities.

"Do you love me?" is the longest command in my vocabulary. While "love" and the questioning tone are the actual operators, my reason for using the phrase is the effect it has on audiences.

To teach the trick to a large animal (using any cue you like), start from a controlled position by commanding, "Sit—Stay." Then give your verbal cue and encourage pooch to place his front paws on progressively higher areas of your frontal anatomy. Suggest this through inviting, encouraging gestures, such as patting your legs, waist, chest and shoulders, as the dog's size suggests.

This may take some time, because a dog has to feel confidence to stand against a person: Not only is he operating with half of his natural balancing system; he can feel vulnerable and exposed. If pooch seems reluctant to bring front feet off the ground, gently grasp the front paws and lift them partway up your frame to the accompaniment of encouragement and praise, bringing him higher as he gains confidence.

Teaching a smaller animal is little different from the foregoing, the main distinction being that more steps are involved. The first is kneeling rather than standing when encouraging your pet to jump. Once he's comfortable standing against you, initiate the game while resting on your heels. This raises you a bit higher, and if you can keep your legs together while maintaining balance in this position, pooch will learn to jump into your lap. That leads to the next step: requiring the dog to jump even higher by seating yourself in a chair. Once he's comfortable with jumping into your lap at that height, encourage him to stand against your chest while you're seated. An instant after your dog jumps into your lap and stands against you, rise from the chair while holding him. Make this move smoothly so as not to startle the little one. After cuddling him for a moment or two, gently set him down, reseat yourself and repeat the process. The final step is encouraging pooch to jump to you while you're seated on the edge of the chair. While it admittedly takes good timing, in one motion stand and catch him *as* he comes up. Now the lesson becomes one of starting from a standing position and enticing your pal to jump higher.

Consider two points about teaching the trick to small dogs. The first is that any canine is limited in how high he can leap. If you're six feet four inches and are working with a Toy breed, doubtless you'll always have to bend your knees to make it possible for the dog to reach you. You must determine how high he can jump and endeavor to meet him there, so to speak. Second, when catching and gently cradling your friend, emphasizing how welcome he is, do so with one hand under his rear and the other high on his back. He feels more secure being held this way than if he were snared with both hands along the ribs.

"Charlie!"

Charlie is the name of my fuzzy little crossbreed. Voiced excitedly, it's also his cue to come to me, but in a certain manner. I've mentioned this adorable pooch at seminars in order to share with the audience his senses of pride and élan, notwithstanding a history of several uncharitable homes interspersed with stays at dog pounds, one of which is where I came across him.

When describing Charlie to students, I observe that after owning him for less than two weeks, he'd come reliably from a distance of twenty feet. Sure, I'm playfully setting the group up, for someone invariably asks, "What's so great about that?" The answer is a rhetorical question: "On his back legs?" When the chuckles abate, I explain that Charlie learned this particular stunt as quickly as any dog I've taught it to, though he tends to back-leg hop rather than run; not that it matters.

This trick is easier taught to one that has learned "Do You Love Me?" because the animal has learned to stand on his back legs. To teach the trick I refer to as "Charlie," first entice your pet to jump against you. Then gently grasp the front paws and step slowly backward a few short paces, keeping pooch against you while excitedly repeating the cue you intend to use. Should the animal try to pull a paw away, encourage him to remain, but not through force. He's likely nervous, not defiant. Get him back upon you and try again, taking fewer and slower steps.

Once he's comfortable with this form of travel, begin to increase speed and take more steps as you move backward. Later, change the format by removing your hands once you start moving away. Later still, back away with such speed that your pet has a little difficulty keeping up. Keep yourself tantalizingly out of reach. Also at this point, raise your hands to the level of your head or higher to suggest that you want your pet to imitate by keeping his front feet up rather than running to you on all four. (If at any stage pooch begins to run to you normally rather than on his back legs, the suggestive posture of keeping your hands high may bring him up on his hind legs.) After a few seconds, allow him to catch up and rest against you.

Make a final adjustment by starting with your pet in the Sit position. Using whatever word or phrase you've settled on, cue him and quickly back away a few paces *as he runs toward you.* Stop and praise sincerely as he leans against you. From here on, the training becomes a matter of gradually lengthening the starting distance between you and your friend.

"Sit Pretty"

I use Sit Pretty instead of the more conventional Beg for several reasons. The first is personal discomfort with telling a dog to beg. True, he'd never be aware of the word's pejorative connotation, but I would.

Second, since I teach this trick by first commanding pooch into a normal Sit, from which he extends into the sit-up posture, *Sit* Pretty reminds him not to leave the Sit position altogether in performing the trick. Last, the phrase seems to enhance an audience's enjoyment and understanding of the true nature of my German Shepherd, Smokey, a certified Police Service K9. This is especially true when he performs the stunt shortly after knocking a 200-pound agitator (bad guy) onto his backside.

To teach this trick, first command, "Sit—Stay." Position yourself at your pet's right side, facing him at a right angle. With a large dog, remain standing; kneel next to a smaller animal. As one move, put your right forearm behind the front legs, cue "Sit Pretty" and smoothly lift the legs upward, helping pooch to balance in position. If necessary, use your left hand against the back to prevent tipping backward or changing from a sitting posture to one of standing on the back legs. When you get your pal into the sit-up position, praise "Good Sit Pretty."

After a few days of such training, once you have your pet balanced in the desired posture, briefly release your hold, but without moving your hands away. Catch and support him in the Sit Pretty position should he lose balance.

Once he can maintain the pose for a few seconds, progress to not physically hoisting him into position. Replace the assistance you've been giving by holding a tidbit just above his nose. Be alert to remove the treat hurriedly should he jump toward it, responding immediately with "No" (spoken, not roared, so as to communicate rather than inhibit), and whisk the hand holding the morsel behind your back. Then command, "Sit," then "Sit Pretty," while again offering the tidbit. Once pooch responds properly, give the treat while praising, "Good Sit Pretty." From this point on, reward with food only intermittently.

Trick for Treat

This stunt has the inherent advantage of heightening canine concentration. It's also one that can often be taught in a single session. Guard-dog trainers should be aware that this trick offers the benefit of teaching the habit of an extremely quick, accurate bite in response to a verbal cue.

In performing the trick, pooch is first commanded to Sit and Stay. A food bit is placed on the dog's muzzle, an inch or so behind the nostrils. The dog must balance it by remaining motionless until cued, "Get It." The animal whisks his nose to one side and snatches the tidbit out of the air.

When teaching this maneuver, keep in mind that while you're better off working your pet several hours after the last meal, don't be instructing him when he's ravenous. The condition of a full stomach or one growling in hunger can bias a dog's perception of the trick toward being more of an act of rigid obedience or of desperation than one of fun.

Tell your pet, "Sit—Stay." Gently grasp the lower half of the muzzle and place a flat food treat upon his snout. As you do, repeat the Stay command. Once the piece is balanced, command "Stay" once more as you slowly remove your hands. When they're a few inches out of harm's way, excitedly tell pooch, "Get It!" (Don't ever make your pal hold the food bit for more than a few seconds—the purpose here is fun, not endurance.)

Most will get the drift and give it the old college try. If the food bit falls away, command "No," and prevent pooch from grabbing it. Direct "Sit—Stay" once more and run through the sequence again. If after three or four tries the dog is unable to catch the tidbit, pick it up and give it to him. We don't want to burn out a dog that is trying his best but simply doesn't have the necessary timing and coordination yet. (If you think it's easy, try it yourself, but use something other than a dog biscuit, lest you crack a tooth.) Praise him for his good attempts and have another go at it tomorrow.

Once your pal has success with the game—and he will if you stick with it—praise sincerely and appreciatively. End the session so that you can be certain your pal finishes on a high note.

"Dog, Take a Letter"

No, we aren't going to teach your friend to take shorthand. He's going to learn to carry a message (or an article) to another person. Dogs get a kick out of this trick. They sense they're performing a useful and therefore enjoyable function, which is indeed the case. A moment ago, I scribbled the name of a soft drink on a piece of paper and gave it to one of my Dobermans with the instruction to "Take It Ron," Ron being an out-of-town visitor watching TV in the next room. A moment later, I heard him tell the animal, "Take It Joel." I'm presently enjoying the soda, and the Dobie took great pleasure from participating.

Start this training by teaching pooch to carry a cloth from you to a friend. Tease briefly with the article, allow the dog to grab it and as he does, the person from whom he took it quickly cues, "Take It (other Person)," while pointing toward the individual. At that instant, the other person begins clapping hands and calling the animal. That's the key to this trick: The object person also gives praise; not just the person sending the dog.

At first, my friend and I were but a few feet apart in a closed room when practicing the activity. Over time, the distance has increased, and the cloth has been replaced with any reasonable article.

"Oops—I Dropped It"

The "it" is most often a piece of laundry, such as a sock or wash-cloth. Oops is the cue for the dog to fetch and carry it. As this can easily happen when carrying towels and such to the laundry area, I have my dogs pick up a dropped article and bring it along. It's an offshoot of a former AKC Utility Dog requirement called the Seek Back, though in this instance I don't teach it with the same degree of structure that I would the ring exercise.

Teaching your pet this useful bit of work is similar to the method of instructing him to carry an object from one person to another, except you don't need an assistant. Confine yourself and pooch in a distraction-free room and playfully entice him with a cloth article. Once you have his interest, drop the object nearby and make a grabbing motion toward it. When he sees that you want it, he'll want it—that's how dogs are. Miss, of course, and allow your companion victory in snatching it up. The instant he mouths the object, say, "Oops," and move hurriedly away, patting your leg as you go and encouraging him to keep up with you.

Should he drop the article, advance quickly toward it, manifesting behavior that suggests you're going to grab it yourself. Trick: When making this approach, shift your gaze repeatedly from canine to object, radiating an atmosphere that you aren't sure if you can beat him to it. When he responds by grabbing it, move away while encouraging him to join you. Should he not pick it up, grab the article and restart the sequence.

Be aware that this technique of grabbing for an object can stimulate an aggressive animal to try to keep you from it by means other than possession. Should your dog display hostility toward you, abandon the trick—at least for now—and straighten the animal out as to just who's running things in the household.

"Trash!"

This command directs a dog to take an object and drop it in the kitchen wastebasket (which is the largest such in my house and is therefore the easiest target). As with the preceding trick, it's useful training. It's also more easily taught to a canine that has mastered the tricks of carrying an object from one person to another and of picking up a dropped article. While it's helpful for him to have already learned the Out command, meaning Let Go, it's not absolutely necessary.

This particular trick should be restricted to animals that are of sufficient height that they can stand with their heads above a waste receptacle's opening. A little dog can be taught to stand on his back feet to expel an article, but he could tip the basket over on himself in the process. That could serve to frighten or anger him, depending on temperament.

While standing near your largest wastebasket (which should be emptied before each of these initial lessons), give your pet a wadded piece of paper and tell him, "Trash." Lead him to the receptacle and guide his head over the opening. Once he's in position, command, "Out." If he doesn't already know this command, tell him, "Out," anyway, and cause the object's release by inserting a finger behind a canine tooth. This will cause nearly any dog to open his mouth momentarily, which is all we need for this trick. As the paper falls away, reward your companion with a dog biscuit.

Hint: Before initiating this training, position the wastebasket a few feet from a wall rather than placing it against one or in a corner. Some dogs are reluctant to walk up to a wall because they sense its limiting properties.

After going through the routine three or four times daily for several days, quit walking your pet to the wastebasket. You may still have to take a few steps to get him moving, but you should be able to fade them out. Then the training becomes a process of increasing the starting distance from the basket.

Once pooch will dispose of an object from one room to another, begin to replace the biscuit concept with praise when he returns. Periodic reinforcement with a treat won't hurt anything, but do so randomly. Praise should be the real reward.

Reflection

For perhaps, if the truth were known, we're all a little blind, a little deaf, a little handicapped, a little lonely, a little less than perfect. And if we can learn to appreciate and utilize the dog's full potentials, we will, together, make it in this life on earth.

Charlotte Schwartz,
Friend to Friend—Dogs That Help Mankind

14

Lessons From the Best Teacher

THIS SECTION examines both traditional and atypical problem-solving approaches and recounts unexpected responses to normal training techniques. The intent is to more fully round your canine understanding while providing some light reading frequently containing not-so-light messages.

Virtually every dog I've known has taught me something or has reminded or made me more aware of some aspect of the human-canine relationship that I otherwise might have failed to appreciate in a fuller sense. Each has contributed in his or her own special way to an album of treasured experiences.

What You Teach Is What You Get

I began the young Doberman's obedience indoors because the training yard was under more inches of snow than he was tall. Because the pup quickly learned Sit on command, I proceeded into Heeling and Automatic Sit. The following day, while heeling through a hallway, the dog sat even though I hadn't stopped. I didn't correct him because no devious intent was exhibited. I attributed the incident to confusion and continued. Moments later, the Dobie did it again: stopped and sat while I was still walking. Feeling befuddled, I praised, "Good Sit," and called off the training to weigh events.

Finally, the dawn creaked. That bright little character had sat at locations where I'd stopped repeatedly during the previous session. He'd learned not just the concept of Automatic Sit but *where* to do it as well.

The experience provided a fuller appreciation of canine patterned-behavior tendencies. It also reinforced the concept—when in doubt, back away and think things through.

Boomerang

The foregoing illustrates a humorous side of patterning. The following is less so. Sometimes a trainer blindly clings to dogma to the detriment of his or her pet.

During a seminar some years ago, a Newfoundland invariably lagged after the Figure Eight's outside turn. (The Figure Eight is an AKC routine in which heeling occurs in an eight-like pattern around two people standing eight feet apart.) The group's sentiment was that the animal was hardheaded, that severe corrections were the order of the day, notwithstanding that weeks of compulsion hadn't effected a cure. After watching the pair heel the Figure Eight a few times, the problem's basis was apparent.

Repetitive, forceful corrections had taught this gentle dog that at a specific spot the handler would always yank the lead. Thus, each time the Newf arrived at that point, she'd freeze for a beat and close her eyes in anticipation of the impending blow. This caused her to lag, which led to another correction, which resulted in more lagging, another correction, ad infinitum.

It was a classic example of canine learned helplessness,* whereby a dog learns to accept abuse as a natural, inevitable consequence of living with humans. Repeated corrections had only frightened and confused the animal, and she was trying to protect herself in the only way she knew.

It's heartbreaking to witness the effects of such mishandling, even when no trainer malevolence exists. My suggestion was to drop the routine for several months, to facilitate the lessening of harmful memories, then reteach it using a new heeling command and with the accent on drive rather than compulsion.

The message here is a simple one: If a given approach isn't working or seems to be backfiring, reevaluate the technique.

*For additional information about this phenomenon, refer to any introductory psychology textbook, such as *Psychology: An Introduction*, by Jerome Kagan and Ernest Havemann (New York: Harcourt, Brace, Jovanovich).

Perhaps Someday

Several clinic attenders were warming up their charges by on-leash heeling. After each command to "Heel," they proceeded to inundate their pets with a barrage of "Watch me. Watch me." Predictably, the dogs were watching everything and everyone but their handlers. Maintaining visual attention was unnecessary: The animals couldn't help but hear where their people were.

Contrary to the professed goal, the practice's effect was to cause the dogs to tune out their owners. I asked one soul how long the group had been using this peculiar method. "About a year and a half." There are times in this business when I ponder taking a bite out of the nearest wall. I mentally shook my head and wondered when they thought the approach was going to work.

I suggested that the group abandon the method and hold a bonfire kindled with the tome that recommended the curious technique. When a dog says an approach is ineffective, hear him out. Pay attention to the obvious. When any authority proclaims that a certain method is effective, all that can be inferred is that the system works for him or her. If you don't achieve immediate and long-lasting results using the same procedure, drop it.

"Platz!"

A seminar student once approached me with a Staffordshire Bull Terrier that couldn't be made to lie down. She'd tried to teach the exercise by commanding the Down position, then pushing on the animal's withers with one hand while pulling downward on the leash with the other. The dog would go down, after a fashion, but then he'd raise right back up. As I knew his handler to be a gentle individual not disposed to abusing any animal and since the Staff seemed amiable toward other obedience, I could rule out canine resentment as a cause.

After working the dog briefly, I was stunned by his lack of aggressive responses. Hostility normally goes hand in hand with prolonged resistance, especially to the Down command. This is because some take the "Down!" order to imply "Lay at my feet, cur!" even though no such message is intended. I was amazed further that the Staff was enjoying the proceedings immensely. I'd push him down—he'd raise back up. No snarls, snaps or growls, just an air of "Care for two out of three falls?"

After a few moments, it came to me what the handler had unknowingly taught this powerful canine: A game of tug-of-war in reverse.

Moreover, pooch was doing quite well at it, winning far more often than losing. During initial teaching, force had been applied steadily rather than abruptly, and therein lay the rub: The technique suggested resistance. Similar to the case with the Newfoundland, I suggested the exercise be dropped for several weeks or months to allow time for negative memory traces to fade, then be retaught via a different method and a new command.

The lessons are that resistance can be taught and that such apparent defiance is not necessarily a sign of stubbornness. If any looks-good-on-paper approach fails, it's usually due to having used the wrong method for the dog in question.

"Platz!": Part Two

Winter was the largest Malamute I'd ever met. Like the Staffordshire in the foregoing section, Winter wouldn't hit the ground, either. Unlike the Staff, which had misunderstood the lesson, Winter comprehended the exercise but not its message. To my knowledge, no one had ever suggested to him that Platz was a demeaning position, yet that's how this dominant three-year-old male seemed to interpret the command. Thus, my first problem was getting him on terra firma so I could deal with the second problem: showing him that no debasing sentiment was intended.

Sensing that pinch-collar compulsion could trigger a fight I might lose, I opted for grabbing the animal's neck fur/skin as a safer method of taking him down. It worked, but only up to a point: The second I'd release my hold, he'd pop back up. Unlike the Staffordshire, though, Winter's message was not one of "Care to try it again?" It was more akin to "You damn well better *not* try it again!" His attitude represented not only disobedience in its purest form but disrespect as well, which is one attitude that cannot be tolerated.

Wishing I were less principled and hoping my hospitalization was paid up, I said, "Platz," grabbed handfuls of Malamute and to the ground we went. No, the "we" shouldn't be "he"—we both went down. Happily, I wound up atop the dog.

What followed was, in retrospect, both scary and amusing. Winter proceeded to attempt to buck me off, and I hung on for dear life: By this point he was snapping at the air, hoping to chomp onto a mouthful of yours truly. It was only my hold on either side of his neck, which by then was not unlike a death grip, that prevented his success.

My training area includes an eight-to ten-foot gently contoured hill. We were at the top of it when the confrontation began and at the bottom when it subsided. The two of us had rolled down the slope in locked-up fashion during the fracas. I hadn't planned such a roller-coaster event— it just worked out that way. For what it's worth, however, to this day that animal is as Platzingest a Malamute as you're likely to meet.

No, I'm *not* suggesting that you ever try such a form of discipline yourself. It was a dangerous experience that could have had tragic consequences. Dumb luck, strength born of fear and good reflexes are what carried the day. My intent in relating this story is simply to underscore my conviction that a trainer must be "one inch tougher than the dog" when compulsion is necessitated (see chapter 5, "Training Guidelines," under "The Rule of Minimal Toughness"). Although the Jack and Jill effect wasn't part of the plan, that's what it took to say to Winter, "Oh, yes, you will!" Now to make him like it, or at least to accept the command without a sneer.

I'd noticed that he was an ardent fan of having his back scratched. Most dogs enjoy such stroking, but this one was something of a junkie. For the next several weeks, whenever he'd plunk himself onto the ground, I began a back massage unparalleled in recent memory. Moreover, that was the only time I'd scratch his spine: Just after he'd Platzed. I then weaned him from constant reinforcement by commanding, "Platz," applying one quick, full-length scratch, "Fuss" for a few steps, "Platz" again and more back petting. Later, I modified this to "Platz," no scratch; "Fuss," a couple of quick steps; "Platz," no scratch; "Fuss," another short distance; "Platz," and a complete back massage. What I was doing, of course, was steadily adjusting the reward into an increasingly sporadic manner, making the "when" element unpredictable. He enjoyed the active praise such that he was willing to respond to intermittent reinforcement, a canine tendency.

"Dumb as a Box of Rocks . . ."

An alternate subheading for the foregoing account could have been "Know Your Dog." Such could also be the subtitle for this section. Some years ago a first-week novice student expressed serious misgivings about his pet's intelligence. "Dumb as a box of rocks" was the simile he used to delineate Sergeant's IQ.

Thus cautioned, I took the leash and proceeded to work with Sarge for a few minutes. By the end of that time, I realized that this year-old male Samoyed/German Shepherd cross would likely be the dog I'd use to demonstrate new material for the class. Stated briefly and with dispassion, he was one of the brighter critters (canine or human) I'd met in many, many moons. Sergeant's impatient owner had made a common misinterpretation: Reading a highly intelligent dog's boredom as stupidity. The animal merely wanted a partner that could keep up with him.

I counseled Sarge's owner to lighten up, to not reflexively judge a canine harshly, to realize that projection is a dangerously easy defense and that absolutes have a way of changing.

Dogs Can't Talk, Or Can They?

Minutes after meeting Smokey I offered to buy him on the spot. The handsome six-month-old German Shepherd was truly a find, embodying all the qualities I seek in a working companion. His owners turned me down, of course, as I would have for the reasons just stated. They did say, however, that were Smokey ever looking for a home, they'd give me first chance.

One afternoon, some three years later, the phone rang. "Are you still interested in having Smokey come live with you?" A cartoonist would have drawn the next panel showing the telephone receiver suspended in midair, with a puff of smoke leading stage right. I set a land-speed record driving to town.

During his first few days with me, I could see that Smokey was slightly befuddled by the change. Given that he'd moved from a home of nearly four years, I viewed his disoriented, somewhat depressed response as normal, understandable behavior. Besides, he was having to make another adjustment: He'd gone from being the only dog in the family to being one of five. He was unsure how he fit in.

His previous owners had sent along his sleep blanket to ease the transition. While it initially provided a measure of security, I noticed that after two or three days, something had begun to bother him about it. Sometimes he'd sleep on it; other times he'd lie near but not on it. Also, during slumber he fidgeted more than is common. After a few days, he cleared things up for me.

One afternoon, after taking a shower, I draped my robe over a chair and began to dress. A minute or two later, Smokey walked to the chair, pulled my scent-laden robe away, dragged it over by the bed and dropped it near his blanket. He then nestled in, onto the robe, gave a weary sigh and went to sleep. He was as relaxed and at peace as I'd seen him since his arrival. For me it was one of the more moving, humbling moments I've experienced.

Analyzing this section could make for a chapter in itself. In brief, I'd not made Smokey's position in the pack clear for him. My own feelings of wanting this fine dog for so long—and then having the great good fortune of his coming to share my home—blinded me to the fact that while reveling in my luck, I forgot to let him know how welcome he was and that he occupied a very special place in my heart. With the advantage of hindsight and knowing Smokey now to a much greater depth than I did then, I can more fully appreciate his "Where do I belong?" anxiety. He did what I should have done, and he gave me a valuable lesson in the process.

"But They're Dumb Animals, Aren't They?"

That's what a gent asked me during a public demonstration of Police K9s. I answered by relating an incident that had recently taken place in my living room.

The newest member of my clan, Cerchie, a five-month-old female Doberman, wanted to repose on the sofa. Alas, there was no room at the inn—the couch was already occupied by three others, and two of them had made it plain to the newcomer that the NO VACANCY! sign was posted. Cerchie stared at them for a moment, sighed and settled for lying on the carpet. After a few moments, she suddenly raised her head and looked toward the front hall. Seconds later, she hopped up and ran at full bark to the door. Of course, the rest of the pack chain-reacted from the couch and followed her.

She had convinced me, too, and I walked to the door, telling the group to hush. As I reached for the latch, I noticed that Cerchie was trotting away from the area. Her behavior seemed odd, but I was more intent on seeing who wanted what than I was on Dobie idiosyncrasies.

I opened the door and greeted no one. The porch was devoid of personage, the driveway was empty and even the county road was bereft of traffic. The rest of the dogs and I walked back into the living room, and there was Cerchie, head on paws, gazing at us from the couch.

Dumb animals? Right!

Lessons Learned Last a Lifetime

This account also concerns a Doberman and a couch. The dog was a massive black male that looked able to whip his weight in wildcats. The pet of a friend, Saber was asleep on the sofa while the owner and I visited nearby.

Soon another dog wandered into the room. Little Bit was a cutie that looked, both in size and appearance, as if he fell off a dust mop. My friend interrupted our conversation and told me, "Watch what happens." The little old dog tottered over to the couch, stopped, stood in place and yipped. Once.

That was all it took. The Doberman—which outweighed Little Bit twelve to one—was flying off the furniture before he was fully awake. The adorable little mongrel then hopped onto the sofa, settled, yawned and was soon asleep. My friend went on to tell me, "Little Bit trounced Saber when he was a pup, and as you can see, he's never forgotten it." It was as clear a demonstration as I've ever seen of the truism that dogs learn for life.

"But the Pitifulness of Myself . . ."

Or so this Toy Poodle had been taught. She was a submissive urinater to the extent that petting or speaking to her caused her to piddle. The owners related she didn't have the problem originally; it had developed a few weeks after bringing her home.

The reactionary piddling grew out of the family's practice of taking audible morning showers first and walking the puppy second. The phrase I recall from Psychology 101 is "stimulus—response." The dog's initial morning contacts with her owners became a cycle of "Damnit! She did it again!" verbal remonstrations and being disdainfully cast outside. After a few weeks of such treatment, the sensitive little animal was predictably a full-fledged submissive tinkler. The pooch felt such fear from a human's approach that she responded by urinating.

To treat the problem, I first enticed the little one to become interested in a play toy. Then I taught her to bark and show aggression toward the object. She possessed much latent fire, élan and toughness.

I was able to bring about a cessation of the submissive dribbling through a combination of the foregoing confidence enhancements and by demonstrating that I wouldn't pet her if she piddled during my approach. I'd walk toward her, and the instant she began to react in her custom, I turned away. It took weeks, but she finally learned she had a choice. She could continue to drive the petter away, or she could clean up her act.

The problem finally cleared up—here at the kennels, that is. It resurfaced once the Toy returned home. Being in her familiar environment caused a reawakening of old fears that reactivated habitual behaviors. Her owners were now more aware and understanding, however, and by using approaches I'd suggested to them, they were able to quickly get her over it.

The messages here are that it's inconsiderate, if not foolish, to neglect a dog's needs, and little dogs are neither pitiful nor timid by birth. That's a condition some unfortunates are taught.

Tincture of Time

A male Rottweiler I trained some years ago had a quirk I've occasionally noticed in other canines, most often in larger ones. In a nutshell, the dog needed a day to assimilate any new lesson. Not a training-session day: twenty-four hours. Whatever I showed him on Thursday would take hold on Friday, no sooner and seldom later.

Was he being resistant or deceitful? No. He was as willing a dog as one could ask for and was incapable of subterfuge. Is such a canine stupid? Hardly. It just took longer for the message to filter through, most likely for reasons that I'd need additional courses in neurology to completely understand. He merely validated an obvious truth: There are quick learners, and there are slow learners. Overall intelligence wasn't germane; the issue was learning rate, not learning ability.

If an animal's eyes read "Out to Lunch," give him a day or even two for absorption. See what happens. You may be in for a pleasant surprise.

The "Delinquent"

The seminar's organizer whispered, "Joel, you ought to know that this dog's been kicked out of two local obedience classes." *Great*, I thought. The wolf hybrid weighed as much or more than I and possessed a set of chompers reminiscent of the alabaster-hued protagonist in the movie *Jaws*. He was dragging his winded, elderly owner, and I saw that until we got the animal under control, the clinic couldn't begin.

Hoping my will was current, I took the leash from the dog's weary partner. It took less than a minute to discover all the answers I'd ever find as to why this animal had twice been given the gate at local classes. Care to guess? If you have an insight, please drop me a note, for to this day I haven't a clue. Except for extreme exuberance—which I showed the owner how to handle—Rocky was as affectionate, bright and willing a dog as one could hope for, the kind of animal that makes a trainer look good. He turned out to be the weekend's star performer. I kept track of how many corrections he received: Three. Save for off-leash work, he *knew* the AKC Companion Dog elements after two days. I later learned that local "expert trainers" had repeatedly pushed Rocky's owner to have the animal put down. It would have been a tragedy spawned of ignorance.

The encounter was rewarding, not just because of the dog's growth—from zero to all-star—but for meeting an owner who would resist pressure from self-appointed sages, choosing to listen instead to his own inner voice about his friend. Such courage is as rare as the degree of Rocky's willingness.

The lessons? Don't judge by appearances or rumors, and when your companion's interests are at stake, stay in his corner, where you belong.

Willingness Revisited

The day Barney went home, I knew his story would be a part of *Dog Logic*. He'd been with me for a month of Companion Obedience, at which he excelled. Golden Retrievers are often fast-learning, steady workers, but this two-year-old male was exceptional. He could have been trained for work ranging from field and/or obedience competition to guide-dog work. He had only one problem, and getting him past it was the devil's own work. It had to do with housebreaking.

Barney's home schedule called for walking him at seven each morning and evening. During the day, he remained in the house while his owners were at work. He fouled the home once and was taken to task over the incident such that there was never a recurrence. So what was the housebreaking dilemma? Read on.

I'd noticed that Barney seldom relieved himself; when he did, however, the output volume was impressive. He often urinated for nearly a minute at a time, and after he evacuated, his run looked as though seven or eight of his friends had stopped by and contributed. During a working session it was fifty-fifty whether he'd drop a load in the training yard.

Perhaps you've deduced why this section is titled as it is. From long periods of confinement and his owner's displeasure over the single goof in the house, Barney had learned that he was not to seek relief until he could no longer stand the pressure. That's why he so often had a movement during training periods: The exercise brought him to the point of no return. The amazing element was that he'd go along with the unintended lesson.

Some might question Barney's intelligence for interpreting the owner's message as he did. I'm more inclined to ponder the insensitivity of those who would permit a canine only two outings daily. Besides, the dog's faculties weren't what led him astray. It was his unsurpassed willingness to abide by the leader's rules as he understood them. In a phrase, Barney redefined the words *willingness* and *loyalty*.

To modify any canine attitude, one must first understand the root problem, which was that the dog had learned shame toward his normal elimination functions. I took the tack of housing dominant males on both sides of Barney's run. Discovering another male nearby, they predictably marked until their bladders ran dry. With Barney present and attentive, I praised them each time they performed. When he followed suit, the praise was effusive and sincere, patting the dividing wall's general area (if not the exact spot) in Barney's view to accent my approval. It took time, but Barney finally adjusted, to the degree that he held his head level when relieving himself rather than down, as had been the case.

I also had a long, long talk with the owners.

When an Owner Can't Hear You

Charger was a nice enough Chow Chow, so long as you never turned your back on him. He was one of three animals over the years for whom I've advised euthanasia. I take no pleasure from such counsel, as I know I'm probably signing the critter's death warrant. My words weren't resented, but they fell on deaf ears.

"He's got some problems, but old Charger would never hurt me," the owner asserted. Four days after that comment, while fueling a wood stove, the dog nailed him, impressively. "Bit me right in the can, he did! Like to drove my head clean through the stovepipe."

The mental images may cause a chuckle, but the situation could easily have reached more tragic proportions. Chow Chows can achieve remarkable jaw compression.

The problem is, how does one discern a Charger from a Rocky, the "delinquent" whose owner was also advised to bag his dog. They were as different as honesty and truth, but it takes experience to see the dissimilarities. Rocky was friendly, outgoing and boisterous; Charger was sullen, withdrawn and paranoid. Rocky liked people; Charger didn't. Rocky could trust; Charger didn't know the meaning of the word.

The moral is, some dogs just aren't "right," and should you find yourself near such an animal, walk away. If uncertain, it's better to pass by a possibly good dog than to risk injury.

In Poker It's Called a Bluff

Like many of her breed, Duchess was a highly intelligent, very trainable German Shepherd. She was friendly, outgoing and devoted to the lady who owned her, a feeling that was obviously mutual. A traffic accident years before had left the owner confined to a wheelchair, and she was wise enough not to teach her pet that she had difficulty controlling her.

Teaching Companion Obedience to this two-year-old German Shepherd wasn't the problem. She internalized the work readily. Preventing her from discovering her leader's limited physical capability to back up commands was the problem. Duchess wasn't an overly dominant bitch, but enough so to have sought the Alpha role had she felt the job was up for grabs.

A local hospital was kind enough to lend me a wheelchair. I taught Duchess I could get out of the conveyance any time I so desired. I further made it clear that it was most unwise to challenge me to the point where I'd actually leap from it. She took the lessons in stride, and they transferred to her owner better than I'd hoped.

A canine knows nothing of such mechanical devices, their purposes or the physical limitations they imply about the users. Other than genetic knowledge (instincts and drives), a dog knows only what he learns.

"Oh, Yes I Will!"

That is what the Saint Bernard seemed to be saying as he glared at me after spilling his food bowl for the second time in as many feedings. He'd flipped it over with a paw, scattering food in all directions. It was a habit he'd developed at home, and his owner wanted it stopped. Of course, my unspoken response as I shooed him outside was "Oh, no you won't!" What I actually told him was "No" (meaning "Never"), which is what I'd said to him after he'd pulled the same stunt that morning. My message was simply "You want to eat? Then don't spill your food." The dog was carrying excess body fat, so I wasn't concerned that missing a few meals would cause starvation. As I'd done earlier, I swept up the food, threw it out and bided my time.

By the following morning, he seemed to have decided, "I believe that this guy means it," because he ingested his nourishment without incident. Two days later, he started to paw the bowl, but a simple "No," accompanied by a pointed glare and fists-on-hips, bent-at-the-waist body lingo marked the end of the problem. It has not resurfaced to date.

You may not have a food spiller, but the principle operating here can be applied to similar situations. Boisterousness in the house, for instance, can be thwarted by temporarily exiling the dog outside, accompanying the temporary banishment with sufficient verbiage to make the point. "You want to play the fool? Do it out there!"

The Urge Is to Comfort . . .

The craving is also to wring the neck of the creep who had terrified Chauncy so, but neither approach would ameliorate the problem. The handsome Great Pyrenees should have radiated pride, but a self-styled "professional" conformation-ring handler (who had sold the dog's owner a bill of goods) had twice thrashed the pooch mercilessly for not placing first. The prolonged beatings had taken place only days apart, leaving the animal emotionally scarred. I enlisted the aid of several friends, but no male human could approach the two-year-old Pyr without inducing hysteria.

An effective way to deal with such a phobia is to appear to ignore the condition, treating the dog normally, with an accent on friendly roughness. For example, when first I cleaned his run, he fled from me in terror, howling hysterically and throwing himself frantically against the concrete-block kennel building in flight. While mentally gritting my teeth in reflection of what the animal must have been through, I cheerfully reacted with "Hi there, pup" and went on with my work as though nothing had happened. In time, his curiosity led him nearer and nearer to me. When I was finally able to put hands on Chauncy, I petted him semiroughly, not in any sort of cuffing or harsh manner but akin to a heated rubdown. It took time, but he learned that a little "violence" was nothing to fear. Babying this fine animal would have been the wrong approach. It would have reinforced the fears, in effect saying, "Yes, that's the right way to react."

When Chauncy went home, he carried his head up and his tail high and waving. He felt good about himself. I was given to reflect that sometimes my vocation can be most rewarding indeed.

The Power of Perceived Applause

Training Kee and Mickey wasn't the problem. The two male Keeshonds were as bright as they were trainable. Building Mickey's confidence was the problem. Not only had his first home been an abusive one, but his friend Kee was very dominant. He enjoyed lording his power over Mickey, which further prevented the younger one from feeling good about himself. While not an excessively dominant dog himself, Mickey was not inherently submissive, either. He had learned to suborn himself, even though such behavior was not in keeping with his genetic predisposition.

You may recall from chapter 5, "Training Guidelines," the gist of the subsection entitled "Praise Can be Shared." The technique entails an after-session reporting to another person of a dog's outstanding obedience efforts moments before. The individual receiving the account responds with approval through exaggerated word, tone and gesture. I used the procedure with Mickey, but instead of seeking out a human for the reinforcement, I enlisted Kee's services.

Following a particularly productive workout, I trotted Mickey over to Kee's run and began the recounting: "Mickey Good Sit," "Mickey Good Fuss," "Mickey Good Stay" and so forth, looking from one to the other during the recital. I'm not saying that Kee understood what was taking place—or that he didn't—but being the easily animated Kees that I knew him to be, he responded to the attention and tone of voice with much hopping about and general enjoyment.

Did it work? You bet! The first time I reported to Kee on Mickey's progress, Mickey seemed a trifle confused and perhaps slightly embarrassed by it all. His attitude was one of "Aw, shucks. 'Twarn't nothin'." By the third such recounting, he could hardly contain himself. His head was up, and his overall countenance radiated pride. Mickey was one happy Keeshond. I think my neighbors may have thought that I'd slipped a bit further—"Now he's talking to *two* dogs, for crying out loud!"— but that was of little concern.

"Because It's There!"

During Wrinks's third or fourth training session, this proud, young Shar-Pei and I happened to heel near the scaling wall, a Schutzhund competition obstacle that can be visualized as 2 seven-by-four–foot sheets of plywood hinged together at one end. When set up, a triangle effect is created. The wall's height at its apex is adjustable, from nonexistent (flat on the ground) to six feet, depending on the angle of positioning. That particular day it happened to be set at full working height.

Just as I began a right turn a few feet shy of the obstacle, with which Wrinks had no previous experience, the animal charged toward, up and over it. I aborted the turn and hurried to time my arrival with his at the wall's other side.

One might ask if I corrected the dog. Answer: of course not. Wrinks didn't know he'd done anything wrong. Upon descending the wall, radiating enjoyment of his feat, he zipped back to my left side, and we continued heeling as though nothing had happened.

Sure, I could have corrected him for breaking from the Heel position and would have had I believed that he knew he'd erred. However, he may have felt that the wall was supposed to be climbed. Remember, at this time he'd had less than a week's training. There was no devious intent, and one of my sacrosanct training rules is "When it doubt, don't." For all I know, he wondered why I didn't crawl over the obstacle with him.

To avoid further misconceptions, we simply didn't heel near the wall during the next few days. Later, I allowed our path to intersect the object, and at one point—while heeling parallel to the obstacle rather than at it—I did prevent him from abandoning my company in favor of a quick up and over. Later still, I taught him to Recall over the wall, which he thoroughly enjoyed.

There's a time to correct, but it doesn't occur until a dog clearly knows what's expected of him. Until that moment is at hand, problems are better deflected than confronted.

Inexplicable Fear

You may remember from chapter 10, "Third Week," that I routinely teach all novice canines to leap over a low jump as part of heeling. In some 90 percent of cases, the dog hops over the hurdle, which is merely an appropriately wide plank propped up on one edge. Pooch enjoys the activity and learns to associate the command Hup with leaving the ground. Very few canines balk at the obstacle. Most that do can be easily coaxed over, and the majority of them come to enjoy jumping. An extremely small number show pronounced rebellion, which is usually born of fear. Taxi was one such.

Each time I tried to heel the otherwise flawless working, one-year-old male Bearded Collie toward the hurdle, he freaked out. While that may not be a very clinical or scientific description of the behavior, the expression communicates the essence of his responses. He'd throw himself away from the jump, flipping around in the air and screaming pitifully. The question, of course, was "Now what?"

After trying on several separate occasions to pacify the frantic, wild-eyed pooch, I decided the best course was to skip the lesson entirely. As with all dogs that I accept for Companion Obedience, Taxi was scheduled to be with me for only a month. I could see I'd need at least twice that amount of time to bring him around, and even then I couldn't be sure that he'd ever get past the fear. It was just in too deep.

This was a very easygoing, nothing-ruffles-his-feathers type of dog, but leading him toward any obstacle caused a Jekyll and Hyde reaction. Compulsion was out of the question, for force should never be applied to a confused or frightened animal, and the pooch's normal sense of play drive was obliterated whenever he was in proximity to the object.

I contacted his owner. She didn't have a clue about his history, having acquired him from people who had since moved away to parts unknown. I felt certain the behavior stemmed from something in his background but had no way of discovering the cause.

Different styles, locations and colors of jumps, different handlers, collars and leashes were tried, along with working at different times and having him observe dogs that enjoyed leaping over the same jump. Food and similar inducements, including the urine from a bitch in season, were used, but nothing helped.

Sometimes the wisest course is to back away, especially when it concerns a peripheral exercise. Taxi's heeling, stays, down on command, recall and finish were all more than acceptable. Had I continued to push the jumping issue, we easily could have lost what we'd achieved. Most canines can be trained, but not all can be fixed.

Like the Setting Sun

The Border Collie Platzed willingly enough—she never came close to refusal; it just took her the better part of a minute to do it. The owner gave the command, and the dog responded, but in stages, as though she were slowly melting into the earth. During the subsequent Stay the otherwise happy worker manifested nervousness to the point of depression.

The owner was a kind person—he obviously cared about his pet—but he had the tendency to rush things, and that was the problem's origin. He'd taught Platz on one day, long-distance Stays the next. His insecure friend had learned the pattern: Platz leads to the pack leader's departure. Because the dog felt anxiety at the owner's leaving, she delayed his disappearance for as long as she could.

We got around the difficulty by adopting a several-week policy of no Stays after a Platz. Stays were later returned to the routine, but the distance element was built very gradually. The owner's hurry-up, let's-get-it-done-yesterday attitude had resulted in an extensive setback, one that could easily have been avoided. More importantly, he'd fallen into the trap of becoming so involved in training for its own sake that he forgot that two beings were involved.

Messages: Take your time; don't forget that's man's best friend at the end of the leash.

Little Miss Echo

Hawkeye was seven months old when I initiated his training. My other German Shepherd at the time was Misty, then barely four months on the planet. Hawk took to the work like the proverbial duck to a puddle. Misty was the audience. Although she could have chosen to involve herself in any number of puppy pursuits during the workouts, seldom was she not near the training-yard fence, silently watching, waiting.

Some months later, I commenced Misty's formal obedience program. As is my custom, I began with leash taming—allowing a dog to receive appropriate pressure for dashing away from the trainer. Of course, before consequential force can be applied, the pooch first has to bound away from the handler. Misty didn't, not once. Moreover, she never strayed from my *left* side.

During our third session, I investigated her reaction to a Schutzhund about-turn, a 180-degree turn initiated to the left. This necessitates that the dog circle behind the trainer, thereby causing the animal to have to instantly decide "On which side do I belong?" Misty zipped accurately to the Heel position as if she'd been practicing the move for most of her life. At this point, I began to wonder if maybe she had.

A day later, I taught her Sit, sort of. As I couldn't seem to shake her from my left side long enough to position her in front of and facing me, which is how I normally teach the Sit, I decided to teach it in relation to the Heel position. The only problem was that when I stopped walking and uttered about one-half of the "S," she sat, beaming up at me and radiating pride. I praised, "Good Sit," commanded "Fuss," took a few steps, halted and realized that she already knew all there was to know about Auto-Sit at Heel, for this time she sat perfectly, without spoken command. Stay wasn't much work, either.

If I ever had any doubts as to the degree of learning a canine can internalize through observation and mimicry, Misty eradicated them. Dogs are tremendous imitators. This is why it's crucial that your attitudes toward your pet radiate what you hope to engender. Send a positive, confident, caring attitude and it'll come back to you. Your pet will imitate it.

Yes, by the way, I congratulated Hawkeye on the fine job he did of training Misty for me.

Mistaken Identity

Here's a final note about the first dog mentioned in this chapter. Much older now, he's earned his AKC CDX degree and his first Schutzhund title and is a certified Police Service K9.

One day, while he was asleep in the back of the house, I went upstairs to locate some dog magazines. Apparently he heard my movements and—not realizing that it was me upstairs—met me in full *Garoof* at the bottom of the staircase as I bounded down the steps. Displaying bared teeth and positioned in his fighting stance, he was decidedly ready to go for it. For just an instant it seemed there might be some truth to the oft-bantered drivel that Dobermans always turn on their owners.

They don't, of course, and as my heart started again, I commented, "Nice technique." By then he'd realized whom he'd confronted, and his response was a Dobie smile, an embarrassed grin of sorts. I petted him, and we walked off for calmer pursuits.

The reason for telling you this story is that some people would have severely thrashed the dog for the purported transgression, even though the animal was responding as he'd been trained. Such hard-liners assert that there's no circumstance which any dog, attack trained or otherwise, should show fire toward *the master*! They're wrong, of course, but even in this particular comedy of errors, they'd advocate taking the animal to task relentlessly.

Such a mind-set is as absurd as it is inflexible. Pooch felt that the home (his territory) had been intruded upon, and he was ready to defend it. In fact, since he knew that I was the only one home, he was ultimately attempting to protect me.

The moral? Should your pet ever show hostility toward you or yours, before you land on him with both feet, make certain you understand the situation. You may never have an event like this one occur, but I know of more than one instance where a dog was beaten mercilessly for snapping at a child despite the fact that the youngster was physically abusing and tormenting the animal.

Endit

I hope you've profited from this section of *Dog Logic*, and that at least parts of it have spoken to you. Writing it has allowed me to revisit many cherished memories as well as others that even today cause a shaking of the head and a muttered "Tsk." All have the potential to teach, though, and to remind.

This Chapter continues in *Advanced Obedience—Easier Than You Think*. I hope to see you there.

Reflection—A Personal Observation

When you enter a room and sit apart from your dog, who is asleep on his treasured scrap of rug, much is revealed about the animal's nature and bonding level when—without even so much as a glance from you in his direction—he arises sleepily to stumble quietly and without intrusion to lie down near you.

Joel McMains

"Well Chattan, I think the thing's writ."

Postscript

I HOPE you've enjoyed *Dog Logic*. I also hope it won't be the only training guide you'll ever read. The dog is at once a simple yet complex creature, and no single book holds all the answers. Much of the joy of working with canines is discovering fresh insights that enrich understanding and yield deeper contact.

Obedience is typically thought of as a distinct training classification, for convention categorizes training under headings such as Obedience, Tracking, Protection, Herding and other specialized functions. In truth, however, all dog work reverts to the general heading of Obedience. A Police K9 responds to protection commands, but in so doing, he's being obedient.

I encourage serious trainers to explore all fields, even those in which they have no intent of active participation. To do so augments overall understanding of *Canis familiaris*. I own nary a ewe, but I know how to teach herding. I'm no hunter, yet I can train a hunting dog. You may never aspire to train for protection, search and rescue or guide work. However, to understand how such forms of training "work," how they say "these things" to a dog, is to increase one's knowledge of what drives our best friend.

I leave you with the following thoughts, which are adapted from the software program *Canis* and are used with permission from Centron Software Technologies, Inc.*

TEN COMMANDMENTS

My life is likely to last ten to fifteen years. Any separation from you will be painful for me. Remember that before you buy me.

Give me time to understand what you want of me.

Place your trust in me—it's crucial to my well-being.

Don't be angry at me for long and don't lock me up as punishment. You have your work, your entertainment and your friends. I have only you.

Talk to me sometimes. Even if I don't understand your words, I understand your voice when its speaking to me.

Be aware that however you treat me, I'll never forget it.

Remember before you hit me that I have teeth that could easily crush the bones of your hand but that I choose not to bite you.

Before you scold me for being uncooperative, obstinate or lazy, ask yourself if something might be bothering me. Perhaps I'm not getting the right food, or I've been out in the sun too long, or my heart is getting old and weak.

Take care of me when I get old; you, too, will grow old.

Go with me on difficult journeys. Never say, "I can't bear to watch it," or, "Let it happen in my absence." Everything is easier for me if you are there. Remember, I love you.

Canis, an excellent program for record keeping, resource information and all-around enjoyment, is available from Centron Software Technologies, Deerfield Beach, Florida, (305) 425-0557.

Glossary

THE FOLLOWING TERMS are defined relative to dog training and related activities. In some instances, the definitions bear scant resemblance to those found in a general dictionary of the English language. The descriptions have been kept as simple and nontechnical as possible.

Active resistance   Overt physical resistance by a dog to a trainer's intent.

AKC (American Kennel Club)   The principal governing body whose primary responsibility is maintenance of purebred dog bloodlines in the United States.

Alpha   Pack leader; number-one animal; the boss.

Animation   Overt canine enjoyment of an event or situation.

Anthropomorphism   Assigning human values and traits to another species. This commonly occurs when one compares the training of dogs to the rearing of children.

Anticipation   Canine performance of a command before the command is given.

Attitude   Canine behavior revealing a dog's feeling toward a command's directive, a situation or an event.

Attraction   Level of canine interest and trust in his handler(s).

Automatic Sit   An obedience basic requiring a dog to sit because an event has occurred. (i.e., during Heeling, the handler has stopped walking; during a Recall or a Retrieve, the animal has arrived at a position in front of and facing the handler.)

Avoidance conditioning Aversive conditioning that allows a subject to avoid totally an unpleasant consequence by reacting properly to an environmental cue. This is a form of *Instrumental conditioning*.

Backsliding A short-lived phenomenon, sometimes occurring during the third to fourth week of obedience training a novice canine, whereby the animal appears to have forgotten all lessons.

Behavior—instinctual Behavior motivated by knowledge with which a dog is born.

Behavior—learned Behavior motivated by knowledge a dog acquires through experience.

Bonding A process that causes a dog to feel deep attraction toward another canine or a human.

Burned out Refers to the attitude of a dog whose training has been so prolonged and repetitious that he's lost interest in the work and may have even developed an aversion toward it and/or toward the trainer.

Carryover effect The positive or negative influence on canine perception of one activity by another.

Challenge the dog A training concept that attempts to bring out a dog's best efforts by making his tasks just difficult enough that he has to work at performing them.

Choke collar A training collar, usually fashioned of steel links, that can restrict and even terminate canine breathing if misused.

CKC (Canadian Kennel Club) The principal governing body whose primary responsibility is maintenance of purebred dog bloodlines in Canada.

Classical conditioning Linking a natural biological response with an unnatural stimulus.

Command A trainer's directive to a dog that calls for a behavioral response on the animal's part.

Communication Exchange of information between two or more individuals, whether human or canine.

Competition Performance of learned behaviors against an ideal standard.

Compulsion External force; pressure.

Concentration Canine- or human-directed attention.

Conditioning 1. Practicing lessons in varying situations. 2. Methods of teaching: See also *Avoidance conditioning, Classical conditioning, Escape conditioning, Instrumental conditioning and Operant conditioning.*

Confrontation Active and overt canine rebellion, usually symbolizing at least a partial struggle for dominance.

Consistency Relating in an unchanging manner to a dog.

Contact Any form of communication.

Contention A canine act that indicates pronounced resistance to a trainer's intent.

Correction A trainer's physical and/or verbal pressure applied in response to a dog's disobedience.

Correction match A competition event that simulates a dog show and allows handlers to correct their dogs in a ring setting.

Critical periods Psychological developmental periods in a puppy's life. See *The New Knowledge of Dog Behavior*, by Clarence Pfaffenberger (New York: Howell Book House, 1963).

Cue See *Command*.

Dead ring The ring of a training collar to which one does not attach the leash. See also *Live ring*.

Deflection Momentarily overlooking low-risk contention or a peripheral aspect of undesirable behavior in order to prevent either from escalating.

Desensitization Systematic lessening of anxiety-producing responses through gradual exposure to stress-producing stimuli.

Distractions Circumstances and/or events that may tempt a dog to veer from the path the trainer has commanded.

Dominance The stance from which a trainer must operate in order to assume the role of *Alpha*.

Dominant Refers to an animal that would rather lead than follow.

Drive 1. Behaviors that seek to satisfy instinctual demands. 2. A training technique based on using natural canine instincts toward certain situations and events. 3. Refers to a dog's degree of attraction toward an activity or object.

Escape conditioning Similar to *Avoidance conditioning*, this is an aversive teaching method that allows a dog to avoid further unpleasant consequences but without an environmental cue.

Fear biter A canine that responds aggressively to normal contact situations.

Fight or Flight The point in the stress cycle where a dog attempts to either attack or flee rather than passively endure the situation causing the stress.

Finish An obedience function through which a dog moves on command to the Heel position.

Fire Canine exuberance, often aggressive in some breeds.

Focus The directing of mental concentration.

Foundational Refers to an obedience lesson that is valuable not only on its own merits but is a necessary element of a subsequent lesson as well.

Fun match A competition event that simulates a dog show.

Gender conflict This concept refers to a dog that doesn't relate well with others—whether human or canine—of the same sex.

Handler See *Trainer*.

Heel position A dog positioned squarely at the handler's left side, with the animal's shoulder adjacent to the handler's left leg.

Heeling A canine's synchronous movement with the handler while maintaining the *Heel position*.

I and the Not-I A dog's view of himself in relation to other beings.

Identifiers Terms that a trainer assigns to objects and beings to create a language with his pet beyond that of commands.

Independent   A dog that prefers to be by himself and on his own.

Instinct   General inborn urges to act in response to basic needs (survival, packlike social structuring etc.).

Instrumental conditioning   An educational method by which a dog develops habits by learning from the consequences of his actions.

Integration   The phase of training during which exercises that heretofore were practiced separately are performed in sequence, thus creating a dog's obedience repertoire.

Intelligence   The ability to thrive and problem-solve in any environment.

Learned-helplessness syndrome   Canine acceptance of abuse as a natural, inevitable and unavoidable consequence of contact with humans.

Learning   A permanent behavioral change resulting from experience.

Learning rate   The speed at which a canine can absorb new material.

Live ring   The ring of a training collar to which a leash is attached. See also *Dead Ring*.

Man work   Training through which a dog learns to contend physically against a human.

Misdirected anger   Canine ire directed toward some object that is not the actual cause of the animal's resentment.

Moment of recognition   The instant at which a dog's aspect communicates "Aha! I understand what my trainer is saying to me."

Name   A dog's appellation, which is more of a positively based attention getter than a definition of self.

Novice   1. Either a trainer or a canine new to training. 2. The first of three obedience-competition levels sanctioned by the American and the Canadian Kennel Clubs.

Open   The second of three levels of obedience competition sanctioned by the American and the Canadian Kennel Clubs.

Operant conditioning   Teaching an active behavior in response to positive or negative stimuli.

Pack   The social structure of a dog's "family."

Pack leader   See *Alpha*.

Passive resistance   Covert canine resistance to a trainer's intent.

Personality   A canine's habitual manner of relating with his environment and with those individuals with whom he has contact.

Pinch collar   A multilinked training device that imparts to a canine the sensation of teeth grabbing his neck.

Play toy   A special toy to which a dog is greatly attracted.

Play work   Concentration-building exercises rooted in positive-reinforcement techniques.

Positive reinforcement   A reward for correct behavior; the term is generally synonymous with praise.

Praise   Affirmation; approval; communicating to a dog that his behavior is as commanded.

214

Pressure See *Correction*.

Put down Canine euthanasia.

Rapport An intangible that says to your pet, "I seek that which I project: respect and oneness."

Recall A trainer's summoning of his dog to a position in front of and facing him.

Reinforcement A stimulus event that results in a behavior change.

Release cue A command that tells a canine that he is on his own for a time; that he is no longer under his handler's direction.

Resistance See *Active resistance* and *Passive resistance*.

Schutzhund A form of competition in which a dog must be proficient at tracking, obedience and protection.

Show lead A lightweight leash commonly used in conformation showing.

Socialization Introducing a dog (usually during puppyhood) to various environments, individuals and experiences.

Stimulus Perceived environmental information.

Stress Sustained factors that create psychological and/or physiological pressure within, or on, an animal.

Submission Acceptance of dominant behavior.

Submissive Refers to an animal that would rather follow than lead.

Teachable moment One of many times in a dog's life when he is more receptive to new learning than during other times.

Temperament Inherent canine psychological soundness and stability.

Temperament testing Systematic evaluation of canine genetically based traits.

Trainable Refers to a dog that is responsive to instruction.

Trainer One who trains dogs.

Training A process through which one takes control of and enhances mutual bonding with a dog by developing a basis for and means of significant communication.

Utility The highest of three levels of obedience competition sanctioned by the American and the Canadian kennel clubs.

Verbal bridge Used to time the moment of a trainer's displeasure with a dog's action(s).

Willingness The degree of inherent and/or learned enjoyment a dog has toward training.

Withers A canine's shoulders.

Work concept Teaching a dog that his obedience is a direct contribution to the pack's welfare.

Working A general term relating to teaching, practicing or applying learned exercises.

Joel McMains sharing some Dog Logic-style rapport with a Rottweiler student.

INDEX

About the Author

JOEL McMAINS has been training dogs professionally since 1976. In addition to offering contract obedience and protection training services, he holds public obedience classes and training seminars. Joel is certified by the P.O.S.T. (Peace Officer's Standards and Training Commission) as a Police Service K9 trainer and instructor for the state of Wyoming. He is retired as the chief K9 trainer for the Sheridan County Sheriff's Department and for the City of Sheridan Police Department. Joel has testified in court proceedings as an expert witness; he taught a course in "K9 Selection, Management, Training, and Deployment" for the Police Science Division of Sheridan College and has been the coordinator of Sheridan County's 4-H Dog Program since 1982.